AN INTRODUCTION
TO
NEW TESTAMENT GREEK

Tutor's
Manual

AN INTRODUCTION TO NEW TESTAMENT GREEK

Tutor's Manual

by
ALISON BALAAM
&
FRANK BEETHAM

Bristol Classical Press

First published in 1994 by
Bristol Classical Press
an imprint of
Gerald Duckworth & Co. Ltd
The Old Piano Factory
48 Hoxton Square, London N1 6PB

A catalogue record for this book is available
from the British Library

ISBN 1-85399-399-9

Printed in Great Britain by
Booksprint, Bristol

Table of Contents

Introduction	page 1	Section 18	page 63
Key and Notes		Section 19	page 68
Section 1	page 6	Section 20	page 71
Section 2	page 11	Section 21	page 75
Section 3	page 14	Section 22	page 79
Section 4	page 16	Section 23	page 83
Section 5	page 20	Section 24	page 86
Section 6	page 23	Section 25	page 90
Section 7	page 28	Section 26	page 96
Section 8	page 31	Section 27	page 100
Section 9	page 35	Section 28	page 104
Section 10	page 38	Section 29	page 110
Section 11	page 41	Section 30	page 114
Section 12	page 44	Susanna	page 117
Section 13	page 48	Bel & the dragon	page 121
Section 14	page 51	Appendix (Grammar)	page 124
Section 15	page 54	Appendix (Accents)	page 126
Section 16	page 57		
Section 17	page 60		

Introduction

This course originated in adult education classes at the University of Warwick. The students are from all walks of life; all they have in common is their desire to read the New Testament in Greek. Consequently the groups are of mixed ability, and include graduates and non-graduates, students who have never learned any other language except English, and others who know several. The central need is to enable them, within about a year, to read the gospels with understanding and with a grasp of the underlying grammatical structure. This is therefore a quick course in *reading* Greek, thorough and comprehensive, and very flexible to suit various teaching and learning styles. It is within the capacity of first year undergraduates and college students, and of older as well as younger learners, of part timers as well as full timers. It requires no previous knowledge whatever except of quite basic English. Above all, it consolidates a sound knowledge of the groundwork of grammar necessary to take full advantage of the texts with commentaries, lexica and parsing aids which are now available on personal computers. Never before has the Greek text of the New Testament been so accessible to English speakers, and never before has an elementary knowledge of New Testament Greek brought such rich rewards.

Fluent and accurate reading requires the constant recognition of the English equivalent of the Greek words before the reader. Furthermore, these words have to be comprehended in groups not necessarily in the natural word order of English. This is difficult for a student whose mother tongue, like English, has few inflections and fairly rigid conventions about word order, and the recognition of the significance of word endings is a skill that is acquired by practice, like the use of the gears in driving a car. Although the pattern of verb endings in Greek is more complex, the noun and adjective endings are also fundamental for the understanding of any sentence, and beginners need to get a feel for them. For this reason, the course begins by introducing the cases one by one with an explanation of their most common functions in a sentence. It is, of course, necessary to learn the grammar by heart and test it as it is introduced; it is often helpful for the tutor to remember that the natural way to test it is to ask "what is the

English for...?" rather than "what is the Greek for...?", since it is recognition of the Greek that the student requires in reading.

There is a danger in concentrating too much on single words, though considerable practice with them is necessary. It is especially helpful to read some original Greek, however little, in order to accustom the students to its natural sequence from the beginning. It is vital to ensure that from the start students have the rhythm and word order of the Greek sentences running through their minds as they translate. Word order in a Greek sentence is seldom arbitrary, and because of the flexibility of the language the word order can express shades of emphasis which are very easily lost in English, especially in a passage where a particular translation has become traditional. For instance, John III, 16[1] οὕτως γὰρ ἠγάπησεν ὁ θεὸς τὸν κόσμον, ὥστε τὸν υἱὸν αὐτοῦ τὸν μονογενῆ ἔδωκεν... is equivalent to "For in this way did God come to delight in[2] the world that his only-begotten son he (actually) gave ..." rather than "God so loved the world that he gave his only-begotten son ..."

The first ten sections are introductory, and therefore there is a separate grammatical summary at the end of section 10 to assist basic revision. Students who have already learned a heavily inflected language such as Latin up to GCSE level may find that they can work speedily through these ten sections omitting some of the exercises, but most beginners will probably prefer to go more slowly for the benefit of consolidation and gaining confidence. It should be stressed that it is not necessary for every student to translate every sentence from Greek to English in order to complete the book satisfactorily; some will find it helpful to do so, but others may well find it possible to omit some sentences, especially in the earlier sections. The earlier sections have been written in the expectation that when tutors and students are satisfied that a point has been grasped well, they will move on, having completed as much of the translation as they need.

---

[1]Section 27, p.227 of *An Introduction to New Testament Greek*.
[2]or "value".

2

Convenient points for revision and consolidation occur at the end of sections 15 and 20; these mark not only possible temporary exit points but also entry or re-entry points for those with some previous knowledge of Greek.

The course is planned to cover the main forms of the present tense before proceeding to the other tenses. This is necessary to give students a firmer grasp of the grammatical structure at each stage so that they may feel confident that they understand the topics they have covered.[3] For this reason historic presents, which are quite common in John, have been translated as present in the key; nevertheless, they often need to be changed to past, once they have been recognised, to conform with normal English usage. However, if it is desired to read a passage containing a verb in the aorist or another tense before the students have reached it in the course, this can be done satisfactorily by simply glossing the verb concerned, as has been done onwards from p. 60 (section 10) of *An Introduction to New Testament Greek*. Students do not find this confusing; if they wish, they can look up a reference to a later section to find a fuller explanation without being worried by having to learn forms which do not yet fit into the grammatical structure familiar to them.

The English > Greek exercises at the end of each section are not an integral part of the course. They are for students who may wish to try writing Greek for themselves, and in practice it will often be wise to advise students to ignore them. At all events, the setting and marking of exercises in translation into Koiné Greek needs very great care. Although Koiné Greek is in many ways more accessible to a beginner than Attic, it is not merely a simplified form of old Classical Greek. Indeed, a glance at Walter Bauer's Introduction to his Lexicon will confirm that both in vocabulary and in morphology Koiné has a separate existence about which much still remains

---

[3]Alteration of the order of the topics is possible, but the students may find it easier to take the topics in the order in which they occur. Though Greek tenses are not all difficult to master and some forms of, for instance, the future, are very easy, this tense does not in practice occur nearly as often as the aorist, which has many ramifications and so needs separate and systematic treatment. (Students using this course for self tuition will find it easier to complete all the sections up to the end of 30 before beginning the Reader.)

to be discovered. An unwary examiner cannot assume that what would be incorrect in Attic will necessarily be so in Koiné Greek, and the safest course for a student wishing to gain a better appreciation of Koiné Greek idiom by writing Greek is retranslation.

The course originated with a group wishing to study St. John's Gospel, and the vocabulary, consisting of 560 words, is based on the most commonly used words in that gospel. It covers conveniently many of the most frequent words in the other books of the New Testament. Verbs come at the beginning of each word list, followed by nouns, pronouns, adjectives and adverbs etc. Parsing practice is an effective check on the accuracy of students' knowledge, and valued by students because the ability to parse is essential to anyone who wishes to compare different translations of a passage in the New Testament. In an examination, parsing and the comparison of the various published translations with each other and the original Greek are arguably a more accurate test of a student's linguistic competence than mere translation of a passage of the New Testament from the original Greek into English .

Groups will proceed at varying speeds. The material is intended to be prepared by the students before each tutorial session; i.e. before the end of the first session it is helpful to go over the material in section 2 briefly, so that the students will have worked through it ready for the second session, and so on. Occasionally the material in a section may have been completed before the end of a session and it may be undesirable to push ahead (though with an experienced group pushing ahead in the early sessions may be right). In case more practice is required, up to section 20 some extra material is offered in the tutor's manual. Some of this is from the Greek Old Testament (Septuagint).

Flexibility is essential in using this course. The pace at the beginning is slow, to get the foundations laid, but it accelerates and after section 20 is probably fast enough even for the most able. The length of the later sections is required in order to treat each tense separately and yet as a whole; what is required for reading Greek (compared with writing it) is the ability to recognise the futures, aorists and perfects that are met

4

frequently and to diagnose the present tense stem of an unknown verb accurately before looking it up in a lexicon.[4] The system of principal parts of verbs which is so useful in learning Classical Greek really breaks down in Koiné because there are so many gaps; for instance, of the principal parts of ἐλαύνω (*I drive*)

ἐλαύνω   ἐλῶ   ἤλασα   ἐλήλακα   ἐλήλαμαι   ἠλάθην

only ἐλαύνω and ἐλήλακα are cited in Bauer's Greek-English Lexicon of the New Testament. This course therefore does not list principal parts but, as well as an indication of frequency of the tenses of the verbs used, has an index of harder Greek words (mainly verb forms), referring to the page where each is introduced. The reader will find that those tenses of Greek verbs which are more difficult to recognise have separate entries in Barclay M. Newman's pocket *Greek-English Dictionary of the New Testament.*[5]

Sections 1-20 are planned to take about one and a half hours' tuition each; and 21-30 about two (though they can be divided). Different groups have completed all 30 sections with 50 hours' tuition (of course, this also represents much individual study time put in by the students). However, it would be unwise to timetable the course for only 50 hours not merely because this would leave no flexibility, but also because the course needs to be reinforced by additional reading, either of a prescribed portion of the gospels or from the reader which is provided as an appendix. Such reading can often be begun well before reaching section 30, if verb forms which remain to be covered are explained as they occur. With this in mind, it is suggested that 75 hours' tuition in all should be allowed for the whole course, including reading practice.

The key contains translations of all Greek passages in *An Introduction to New Testament Greek* except the passages in the reader which come from the New Testament.

---

[4] The assistance of a parser is available with several software programmes.
[5] The compound aorist ἀπήλασε is found at Acts XVIII, 16.

Key and notes

Section 1

Pronunciation

The sound of ancient Greek speech has been illustrated by W.S. Allen and D. Raeburn in their cassette *Speaking Greek*, available for use with Jones & Sidwell's *Reading Greek* (Cambridge), which demonstrates both the melodic (pre 300 B.C.) and the dynamic way of speaking Classical Greek.[1] However, koiné Greek underwent prolonged changes in pronunciation in the following centuries, and there were also probably differences in regional pronunciation, many details of which are now lost.[2] The accurate reproduction of the pronunciation of koiné as spoken in 1st century Antioch, for instance, is probably now impossible, but it is not hard to find equivalents to the Greek letters so that one can pronounce Greek words to oneself. The letters, as set out on pp. viii and ix, need little explanation. Here are a few additional hints:

α can stand for short a (as in *cat*) or long a (as in *castle*).

γ is hard, as in *goat*.

η had been pronounced in Classical Greek like *ai* as in *hair*,

and by the time of Medieval Greek would be pronounced like *ee* as in *queen*.

θ is conveniently pronounced as *th* in *theatre* by most English

speakers, but was probably actually pronounced more like *Th* in *Thomas*.

ι can be either long (as *ea* in *bead*) or short as (*i* in *pin*).

υ can also be long or short. It was probably pronounced

more like the German *ü* as in *müller* than like the English *u* as in *put* or *flute*.

---

[1]See E. Phinney in Jones & Sidwell, *The Teachers' Notes to Reading Greek*, pp. 10-11 and *Reading Greek* (Grammar, Vocabulary & Exercises volume) p.264.
[2]See R. Browning, *Medieval and Modern Greek*, pp.31-35.

Section 1

σσ is pronounced *sh* as in *she*. (In Classical Athens ττ was often found where koiné has σσ. So in koiné the word for *sea* is θάλασσα, but in Attic it is θάλαττα.)[3]

Key

page 2

Moses (or Moyses)		Nathanael	Nazaret[4]
Capernaum[5]	Nicodemos	Sale(i)m	Samar(e)ia
Cana	Sychar	Bethesda	Tiberias
Bethle(h)em	David	Siloam	Lazaros
Solomon	Mary (Maria)	Caiaphas	Martha
Barabbas	Caesar	Thomas	Sion

(a)

Khristos (Christ)   Pharisaioi (Pharisees)   Petros (Peter)
Galilaia (Galilee)   Samareitis (Samaritan-ess)   Messias (Messiah)
Sabbaton (Sabbath)   Philippos (Philip)   Satanas (Satan)
Nazoraios (Nazarene)   Pilatos (Pilate)   Levites (Levite)

(b)

cosmos   manna   crisis skhisma (schism)
prophetes (prophet)   blasphemia (blasphemy) synagoge
                                                        (synagogue)

page 3
(c)

thermos	film	taxi	tennis
drama	souvenir	mixer	dynamo
starter	piano	salami	monastery
party	cake	traveller's cheque	cricket

---

[3]Not invariably; for instance, koine has ἐλάσσων for "less", whereas Attic has ἐλάττων, but both koine and Attic have ἐλαττόω for "I make smaller".
[4]Nazareth
[5]Capharnaoum

Section 1

paté   picnic   sandwich   banana

(d)
mousiké (music)   geologia (geology)   zoologia (zoology) pseudo
biographia (biography)   logikos (logic)   catastrophe
baptisma (baptism) teleskopos (telescope) metropolis pneumatikos
(pneumatic)

mekhanikos (mechanic)

cathedra

Appendix
(e)
Sikelia (Sicily)   Sophocles   Minos   Demosthenes
Messene   Korinthos (Corinth) Marathon   Sparte (Sparta)
Philadelphia   Kupros (Cyprus)   Plato(n)   Thermopylae
Macedonia   Thessalonike[6]   Suria[7]   Felix
Miletus   Kornelios (Cornelius) Demetrios (Demetrius) Lydia
Klaudios Kaisar (Claudius Caesar)

page 4
(f)
Parisi (Paris)   Londino (London)   Rome   Germania
                                               (Germany)

Belgio (Belgium)   Bulgaria Brettania (Britain)
                                               Tourkia (Turkey)

Crete   Rumania   Kanadas (Canada)
                                               Scandinavia

Giorgios (George)   Shakespeare   Febrouarios   Martios
Maios   Septembrios   Noembrios   Decembrios[8]

---

[6]Thessalonica
[7]Syria
[8]The modern Greek names of the other months are: Ἰανουάριος, Ἀπρίλιος, Ἰούνιος, Ἰούλιος, Αὔγουστος Ὀκτώβριος. They have been omitted because breathings are not introduced until section 2.

8

Section 1

Σιλας	Ταβιθα	μαμμων
Γεννεσαρετ	Βαρναβας	Κλαυδια
Πρισκιλλα	Σαμψων	Γαβριηλ
Δαμασκος	Φρυγια	Γαλατια
Καισαρεια	Ταρσος	Δανιηλ
Βαρτιμαιος	Βηθανια	Κιλικια
Στεφανος	Τιμοθεος	

Additional practice

Books of the Old & New Testaments (including the Apocrypha)

Capital letters	Small letters	
ΓΕΝΕΣΙΣ	Γένεσις	*Genesis*
ΛΕΥΙΤΙΚΟΝ	Λευϊτικόν	*Levitikon*
ΔΕΥΤΕΡΟΝΟΜΙΟΝ	Δευτερονόμιον	*Deuteronomion*
ΚΡΙΤΑΙ	Κριταί[9]	*Kritai (Judges)*
ΡΟΥΘ	Ρούθ	*R(o)uth*
ΒΑΣΙΛΕΙΩΝ	Βασιλειῶν[10]	*Basileion (of kings)*
ΤΩΒΙΤ	Τωβίτ	*Tobit*
ΜΑΚΚΑΒΑΙΩΝ	Μακκαβαίων	*Maccabaion (of Maccabees)*
ΨΑΛΜΟΙ	Ψαλμοί	*Psalmoi (psalms)*
ΠΑΡΟΙΜΙΑΙ	Παροιμίαι[11]	*Paroimiai (proverbs)*
ΣΟΦΙΑ ΣΟΛΟΜΩΝΤΟΣ	Σοφία Σολομῶντος[12]	
	Sophia Solomontos (Wisdom of Solomon)	

---

[9]Judges
[10]Of things about kings
[11]Proverbs
[12]Wisdom of Solomon

9

Section 1

ΜΙΧΑΙΑΣ	Μιχαίας	*Mikhaias (Micah)*
ΝΑΟΥΜ	Ναούμ	*Naoum (Nahum)*
ΖΑΧΑΡΙΑΣ	Ζαχαρίας	*Zakharias (Zechariah)*
ΚΑΤΑ ΜΑΘΘΑΙΟΝ	Κατὰ Μαθθαῖον	*Kata Matthaion*
		according to Matthew
ΚΑΤΑ ΜΑΡΚΟΝ	Κατὰ Μᾶρκον	*Kata Markon*
ΚΑΤΑ ΛΟΥΚΑΝ	Κατὰ Λουκᾶν	*Kata Loukan*
ΠΡΟΣ ΚΟΡΙΝΘΙΟΥΣ	Πρὸς Κορινθίους	*Pros*
		Korinthious (to the Corinthians)
ΠΡΟΣ ΓΑΛΑΤΑΣ	Πρὸς Γαλάτας	*Pros Galatas*
ΠΡΟΣ ΦΙΛΙΠΠΗΣΙΟΥΣ	Πρὸς Φιλιππησίους	
		Pros Philippesious
ΠΡΟΣ ΘΕΣΣΑΛΟΝΙΚΕΙΣ	Πρὸς Θεσσαλονικεῖς	
		Pros Thessalonikeis
ΠΡΟΣ ΤΙΜΟΘΕΟΝ	Πρὸς Τιμόθεον	*Pros Timotheon*
ΠΡΟΣ ΤΙΤΟΝ	Πρὸς Τίτον	*Pros Titon*
ΠΡΟΣ ΦΙΛΗΜΟΝΑ	Πρὸς Φιλήμονα	*Pros Philemona*
ΠΕΤΡΟΥ	Πέτρου[13]	*Petrou (of Peter)*

---

[13] Of Peter.

Section 2

(a)

Jesus	Israel	Annas	Arimathaea
amen	rabbi	Jacob	Joseph
Abra(h)am	Judas	hosanna	hallelujah

(b)

Joannes(John)	Andreas(Andrew)	Iscariotes[1]	angelos(angel)
the Judaeans (the Jews)		Esaias (Isaiah)	Hellenisti[2]
Romaisti[3]	eucharistia[4]	ecclesia	hypocrites[5]

(c)

Magdalene	Golgotha	Isaac	Rachel
Ruth	Decapolis[6]	Beelzebub	Adam
Caesareia	Samuel	Michael	Gamaliel

(d)

Zebedaios	Zacharias	Herodes (Herod)	Bartholomaios (Bartholomew)
Aigyptos (Egypt)	John the Baptist		the Sadducees

---

[1] Iscariot. Bauer notes that the meaning is obscure, but is usually taken as "from Kerioth" (in southern Judaea). Others connect it with σικάριος (Latin *sicarius*) = "assassin".

[2] in Greek

[3] in Latin

[4] eucharist; thanks.

[5] hypocrite "pretender" (in Classical Greek it meant "actor" (on the stage).)

[6] "Ten cities", the name of a territory east of Jordan which was originally a league of ten cities.

Section 2

(a)
Who are you?   I am not the Christ.
Are you Elias?   No. (literally, I am not.) Are you the prophet? No.
Who is the man?
It is the Sabbath. [7]
(page 8) The word is true.
You are a disciple.
Who is it, Lord?

(b)
1. Who is Joseph? He is a man. 2. Who is Caiaphas? 3. Who is Mary? 4.
Who are you? Are you a disciple? No. (literally, I am not) 5. Mary is not a
disciple.
6. Lazarus is a Jew.
7. Who are you? I am not David.
8. Solomon is not a prophet.

(Optional exercise)

Ἀννα   Ἡλλας   Ἑρμας
Ἡλιας   Ἀσια   Ῥωμη
Ἐλισαβετ   Ἰταλια   Φιλημων
Ἀμφιπολις   Ἀπολλωνια   Ἀθηναι
Ῥοδη   Χριστιανος
ἀποκαλυψις

1. ὁ λογος οὐκ ἐστιν ἀληθινος.
2. ὁ ἀληθινος μαθητης εἰμι.
3. οὐκ ἐστιν (ἡ) Μαρια.
4. τις εἰ;
5. οὐκ εἰμι ἀξιος.
6. ἰδου ὁ ἀνθρωπος.

---

[7]"The" is often omitted with σάββατον. Zerwick & Grosvenor note that the Hebrew
word *shabat* means "rest".

Section 2

Additional practice

ΕΞΟΔΟΣ	Ἔξοδος	*Exodos (Exodus)*
ΑΡΙΘΜΟΙ	Ἀριθμοί	*Arithmoi (Numbers)*
ΙΗΣΟΥΣ	Ἰησοῦς	*Jesous (Joshua)*
ΕΣΔΡΑΣ	Ἔσδρας	*Esdras (Ezra)*
ΕΣΘΗΡ	Ἐσθήρ	*Esther*
ΙΟΥΔΙΘ	Ἰουδίθ	*Judith*
ΕΚΚΛΗΣΙΑΣΤΗΣ	Ἐκκλησιαστής	*Ecclesiastes*
ΙΩΒ	Ἰώβ	*Job*
ΩΣΗΕ	Ὠσηέ	*Osee (Hosea)*
ΑΜΩΣ	Ἀμώς	*Amos*
ΙΩΗΛ	Ἰωήλ	*Joel*
ΑΜΒΑΚΟΥΜ	Ἀμβακούμ	*Ambakoum (Habbakuk)*
ΗΣΑΙΑΣ	Ἡσαΐας	*Isaiah*
ΙΕΡΕΜΙΑΣ	Ἰερεμίας	*Jeremiah*
ΙΕΖΕΚΙΕΛ	Ἰεζεκιήλ	*Ezekiel*
ΚΑΤΑ ΙΩΑΝΝΗΝ	κατὰ Ἰωάννην	*kata Ioannen (according to John)*

ΠΡΑΞΕΙΣ ΑΠΟΣΤΟΛΩΝ Πράξεις Ἀποστόλων
Praxeis Apostolon (Acts of the Apostles)

ΠΡΟΣ ΕΦΕΣΙΟΥΣ	πρὸς Ἐφεσίους	*pros Ephesious (to the Ephesians)*
PROS EBRAIOUS	πρὸς Ἑβραίους	*pros Hebraious (to the Hebrews)*
ΙΑΚΩΒΟΥ	Ἰακώβου	*Iakobou (of James)*
ΙΩΑΝΝΟΥ	Ἰωάννου	*Ioannou (of John)*
ΙΟΥΔΑ	Ἰούδα	*Iouda (of Jude)*
ΑΠΟΚΑΛΥΨΙΣ ΙΩΑΝΝΟΥ		Ἀποκάλυψις Ἰωάννου

Apokalupsis Ioannou (Apocalypse of John)

ὁ θεὸς φῶς ἐστιν καὶ σκοτία ἐν αὐτῷ οὐκ ἔστιν. (I John 1,5)
God is light and darkness in him (there) is not.
Additional words: (τὸ) φῶς = (the) light
                (ἡ) σκοτία = (the) darkness
                ἐν αὐτῷ = in him

Section 3

page 10
1. You are a thief. I am not a thief.
2. Is the disciple a bandit? 3. The disciple is a bandit.
4. Simon is not a slave.
5. Barabbas is a thief and a bandit.
6. Is Zebedee a prophet? No. (literally, he is not.)

I am the door.
I am the road,[1] the truth and the life.
You are Simon the son of John.
What is truth?
pages 11-12
1. The true word, the dear (or friendly) disciple, the bad deed, the pure truth, the bad vine.
2. Mary is friendly.[2] 3. The son of John is a disciple.
4. The bandit is a bad man.
5. The pure life is fine (or "noble").
6. The evil deed is not (a) pure (thing).
7. The book is true.
8. The thief is evil! 9. The truth is good!

I am the true vine.
I am the noble (?) good(?) shepherd.[3]
page 13
1. The friendly men (= the friends). 2. The friendly women (= the friends). 3. The bad disciples. 4. The pure words. 5. The fine (or noble)

---

[1] See C.K. Barrett, *The Gospel according to St. John*, p. 458. ἡ ὁδός sometimes also means "way of life".

[2] or "Maria is dear". φίλος has both the active and the passive meaning. Greek words do not have exact equivalents in English and often cover a range of English meanings. It will often be a matter for discussion which meaning is most appropriate for a particular context.

[3] Bauer gives καλός the meanings "excellent" or "blameless" in this passage.

Section 3

sons. 6. The friendly deeds. 7. The bad roads. The friendly bandit. 10.
The beautiful books.

1.<u>We</u> are blind. 2.Are <u>you</u> friends? 3.Yes. (literally, we are.) 4.The
disciples are not thieves. 5.Mary and Ruth are beautiful.[4] 6.The words are
not true. 7.You are pure. 8.The noble slave and the blind prophet are
disciples. 9.The roads are bad.

<u>You</u> are pure.
<u>You</u> are my friends.
Truly, you are my disciples.

Optional exercise.
1.προφηται κακοι εστε.
2.άληθως κλεπται ούκ έσμεν· μαθηται καλοι έσμεν.
3.ό κλεπτης και ό ληστης φιλοι είσιν.
4.έγω είμι ή άμπελος.
5.σκληρος εί άνθρωπος.
6.τις άρα έστιν ό πιστος δουλος;

Additional material

'Υμείς έστε τό φώς του κοσμου. (Matthew V, 14)
<u>You</u> are the light of the world.
οίδά σε τίς εί, ό άγιος του θεου. (Luke IV, 34).
I know (you) who you are, the holy one of God.
New words:
του κοσμου = of the world οίδα = I know σε = you ό άγιος = the holy
one του θεου = of God.

---

[4] "Mary and Ruth are excellent" would be less likely because καλός = "excellent" usually
qualifies a generic like "shepherd" rather than the name of an individual.

15

page 16
1.We say. 2.You say. (singular) 3.He/she/it says. 4.Does he/she/it say?
5.He/she/it does not say. 6.Peter says. 7.Do they say? 8.They do not say.
9.Who says? 10.The Pharisees say. 11.You do not say. (plural) 12.The
disciples baptise.[1] 13.The prophets do not baptise. 14.We baptise. 15.Do
we baptise?[2]
page 17
Truly, truly, I say to you.
And Jesus says to him.
Nicodemus says to them.
And they say to her.
Jesus says to her.
The disciples say to him.

1.We see. 2.You hear. (singular). 3.You want (or wish). (plural) 4.They
write. 5.The disciple hears. 6.The prophet sees. 7.The teachers write.
8.We are not waiting (*or*, We do not stay.) 9.He/she/it doesn't send.
10.You don't hear. (plural) 11.You don't undo. (singular)
12.The prophet doesn't write.
13.The thief isn't waiting. 14.The sons believe (*or*, have faith).
15.Aren't you waiting, bad slaves?
16.The bad men aren't waiting.
17.The blind don't see.
18.The bad disciple doesn't believe.
Rabbi, where are you staying?
page 18
1.We are speaking, you are listening. 2.I am writing, you are looking.
3.The prophet is speaking, his friends believe (him).
4.Do you believe, evil disciples?
5.The blind man hears and believes.

Are you the teacher?

---

[1]or "The disciples are baptising."
[2]or "Are we baptising?"

Section 4

You do not have faith in me (*or*, You do not trust in me).
You do not hear (listen).
Do you believe? (*or*, Do you have faith?)
Where are you from?

<u>pages 19-20</u>
1.The disciple himself. 2.The slave himself. 3.The book itself. 4.The vine itself. 5.The deed itself. 6.The deeds themselves. 7.The bandits themselves. 8.The words themselves. 9.The roads themselves. 10.The books themselves. 11.The prophet himself is baptising. 12.The truth itself is pure. 13.The disciples themselves are waiting (*or*, remain). 14.I myself am writing (*or*, I myself write).

<u>page 20</u>
1.The deeds are fine. 2.The lads are listening (*or*, The lads hear). 3.The children are writing (*or*, The children write) . 4.The lads are friendly. 5.The lads are friendly. 6.The children are waiting. 7.The child is waiting. 8.The deed is evil (*or*, The work is bad). 9.What are the children writing?

<u>page 21</u>
You are already pure.
Do you believe now?
I am not alone.

<u>pages 21-22</u>   I
1.You believe.(singular) 2.You wait.(*or*, You are waiting) (plural) 3.They write (*or*, They are writing). 4.We send (*or*, We are sending). 5.<u>I</u> hear. 6.What do you want? (singular) 7.What do you say? (*or*, What are you saying?) (singular) 8.What do you want? (plural) 9.I see (*or*, I am looking). 10.We undo (*or*, We are undoing).[3] 11.You baptise. (singular) 12.He/she/it says. 13.You remain.(singular) 14.They baptise. 15.We hear. 16.He/she/it writes. 17.<u>We</u> have faith. 18.<u>We</u> remain. 19.<u>You</u> wish. (plural) 20.<u>I</u> send. 21.<u>You</u> say. (singular) 22.I do not baptise. 23.You do not stay.(singular) 24.He/she/it doesn't hear. 25.<u>We</u> do not believe. 26.<u>You</u> are not willing. (plural) 27.You send. (plural) 28.The prophet says. 29.The disciple writes. 30.The slave is writing. 31.Is the son writing? 32.The thief writes. 33.The prophets are waiting (*or*, The prophets remain). 34.The prophets are waiting (*or*, The prophets remain).

---

[3]From now on, the alternative form will be assumed.

17

Section 4

35.Are you staying, O disciples? 36.Don't you hear? (*or*, Don't you listen?) (singular) 37.The bad disciple doesn't listen. 38.The blind man doesn't stay. 39.What do you want, bad slaves? 40.The prophet himself is listening. 41.The books themselves are true. 42.The lads see. 43.The deeds themselves are not bad.

II

1.You send. (singular) 2.You see. (plural) 3.He/she/it stays. 4.They baptise. 5.We say. 6.<u>You</u> remain. (singular). 7.<u>I</u> hear. 8.They say. 9.What are they saying? I don't hear. 10.What do you say? (singular) 11.What do you say? (plural) 12.What do you say, prophets? 13.The sons stay. 14.The thief does not stay. 15.The disciple writes. (*or*, The disciple is writing.) 16.Is the disciple writing? 17.The prophet is not writing. 18.Aren't the disciples writing? 19.The sons are listening. 20.Are you listening, men? 21.The bad man doesn't listen. 22.Do you hear, blind men? 23.We hear, and believe. 24.The blind man is a disciple. 25.Is the thief a disciple? 26.Are you disciples, Pharisees? 27.We are not disciples. 28.<u>We</u> are disciples, <u>you</u> are thieves. 29.<u>We</u> are not thieves. 30.Do <u>you</u> hear and believe? 31.The friends are blind. 32.The desert is beautiful. 33.The prophet is speaking; the disciple stays and listens. 34.The thief himself has faith. 35.The desert itself is beautiful. 36.Are the children listening? (*or* Do the children hear?) 37.The lads believe (or, The lads have faith). 38.Are you yourselves listening, Mary and Ruth? We ourselves are listening. 39.Are you yourself looking? Yes (literally, I am looking).

Optional exercise.
1.αὐτος ὁ διδασκαλος μενει or ὁ διδασκαλος αὐτος μενει.
2.ἡμεις βλεπομεν· ὑμεις γραφετε. (or συ γραφεις).
3.τα παιδαρια οὐκ ἀκουει.
4.Τι θελετε;
5.εἰπον ὑμιν και οὐ πιστευετε.
6.ἐγω εἰμι αὐτος.

18

Section 4

Additional material.

καὶ (Ἠλι) εἶπεν Ἀνάστρεφε, κάθευδε, τέκνον, καὶ ... ἐὰν (ὁ κύριος) καλέσῃ σε ... ἐρεῖς Λάλει, κύριε, ὅτι ἀκούει ὁ δοῦλός σου. καὶ ἦλθεν κύριος ... καὶ εἶπεν Σαμουηλ Λάλει, ὅτι ἀκούει ὁ δοῦλός σου. καὶ εἶπεν κύριος πρὸς Σαμουηλ, Ἰδου, ἐγὼ ποιῶ τὰ ῥήματά μου ἐν Ισραηλ ὥστε παντὸς ἀκούοντος αὐτὰ ἠχήσει ἀμφότερα τὰ ὦτα αὐτοῦ.

(I Kings (Septuagint) III, 9-11)

New words: εἶπεν = (he/she/it) said ἀνάστρεφε (imperative) = go back!, turn back! κάθευδε (imperative) = go to bed! ἐάν = if καλέσῃ = calls (the tense is aorist subjunctive; see sections 18 and 25) σε = you (object) ἐρεῖς = you will say (future of λέγω, ε-contracted tense; see sections 11 and 23) λάλει (imperative) = speak! ὅτι = because σου = of you ἦλθεν = (he/she/it) came Ἰδού = behold (strong aorist middle imperative (section 27); the aorist active imperative form is used in section 6 (p.32)) ποιῶ = I do, perform τὰ ῥήματά μου = my words, my sayings (*literally*, the sayings of me) ἐν = in ὥστε = so that πάντος ἀκούοντος = of every hearer ἠχήσει = shall resound (shall echo)[4] ἀμφότερα = both τὰ ὦτα αὐτοῦ = the ears of him (i.e., his ears).

And (Eli) said, "Go back, go to bed, child, and if the Lord calls you, ... you will say 'Speak, Lord, because your slave is listening.'" And the Lord came and Samuel said, "Speak, because your slave is listening." And the Lord said to Samuel, "Look, I am performing my sayings in Israel so that of every one who hears them (literally, of every hearing-them person) both his ears will resound."

---

[4]This is the future of ἠχέω = I thunder.

19

Section 5

pages 24-25
They do not have wine. (*or*, They have no wine, *or*, They haven't any wine).
On the next day ... Jesus finds Philip.
Philip finds Nathanael.
I don't have a man (or, I have no man).
Every man first puts out the good wine.
page 25
1.We see the truth. 2.They are writing a book. 3.The bad slave doesn't have (any) bread (or, The bad slave has no bread). 4.Does the prophet say a noble word? 5.The prophet is sending a disciple. 6.Don't you find him? 7.A good deed is everlasting. 8.Are you listening? (or, Do you hear?) 9.The disciple discovers the truth. 10.Do we have eternal life?
11.Where is Ruth? Don't you see her?
12.I don't see the baked fish. Do _you_ have it?
page 26

1.We see the disciples.	2.We see the actions.
3.The roads are bad.	4.Judaea has bad roads.
5.They have no baked fish.	6.Don't they have bread?

7.Where are the books? We don't find them.
8.Where are the men? We don't see them.
9.I don't want the baked fish. Do _you_ want them?

He has five loaves and two baked fish.
I am speaking the truth to you.[1]
They see a coal fire laid and baked fish laid on top and (a loaf of) bread.
page 27
1.I see you. 2.Do you see me? 3.Are _you_ listening? (or, Do you hear?) 4._We_ have the truth. 5.Are they sending us? 6.We see you. 7._You_ have no bread. 8.The teacher doesn't see you. 9.Where are you staying? 10.Does the prophet see you? 11.The disciples don't see me. 12.I don't find the wine.

---

[1]The personal pronouns are often put in to contrast the points of view of two different (sets of) people. When this happens, it is often unnecessary to underline in English to mark the emphasis.

Section 5

Optional practice:
1.Do you see the wine? Yes. (literally, I see the wine.) Is the wine good?
No. (literally, It is not.) The wine is not pure.[2]
2.We have bad bread, Nathanael. Have you a baked fish? Yes. (literally, I have a fish.) Is the baked fish good? No. (literally, It is not.) Neither the baked fish nor the bread is pure.
3.Do you find the door? Yes. (literally, We find the door.)
4.Do the prophets have wine? 5.No. (literally, They don't have wine.)
6.Do you see Philip? 7.Philip is writing.
8.The child has five baked fish.
9.Philip sees Mary. 10.Philip sees Mary.
11.The thief finds the baked fish. The thief has the baked fish.
12.We don't see the prophets. 13.You are blind, O men.
14.The prophet is writing two books. They are truthful.[3]
15.Philip has bad friends. They are bandits.
16.Do you have good loaves, Ruth and Mary? We do, (literally, We have (some)) and five baked fish.
17.The prophet doesn't see the thieves. Doesn't he see (them)? No, (literally, He doesn't see them) because he is blind.

Optional exercise.
1.ὁ κλεπτης τον καλον οἰνον οὐχ εὑρισκει.
2.ἡμας οὐ βλεπετε (or ἡμας οὐ βλεπεις). 3.τα τεκνα τας βιβλους θελει.
4.οὐκ ἐχετε ζωην.
5.λεγουσιν· δαιμονιον ἐχει.
6.αὐτος Δαυιδ λεγει αὐτον κυριον.

---

[2]καθαρός can mean "ritually pure", i.e., fit for use in the temple (cf. Romans xiv, 20 and Bauer, p.388).
[3]ἀληθινός and ἀληθής both mean "dependable" as well as simply "true".

Section 5

Additional material

Ἐγώ εἰμι τὸ ἄλφα καὶ τὸ ὤ, λέγει κύριος ὁ θεός. (Revelations I, 8)
I am alpha and omega, says the Lord God.
Κύριος ποιμαίνει με. (Psalm 22 (Septuagint), verse 1)
The Lord shepherds me.
ποιμαίνω = I shepherd.

καὶ ἐφύτευσεν κύριος ὁ θεὸς παράδεισον ἐν Εδεμ ... καὶ ἔθετο εκεῖ τὸν ἄνθρωπον ... ἐργάζεσθαι αὐτὸν καὶ φυλάσσειν. (Genesis II 8 & 15)(Septuagint)
And the Lord God planted a garden in Eden, and placed the man there to work it and guard (it).
ἐφύτευσεν = (he) planted ὁ παράδεισος = the garden[4] ἔθετο = he placed (aorist middle of τίθημι - see section 27 and conspectus of grammar, p.339) ἐργάζεσθαι = to work αὐτόν = it (masc.) φυλάσσειν = to guard.

---

[4]παράδεισος, from the Persian *pairidaeza* ("enclosure"), originally meant a formal garden or park belonging to a Persian king or nobleman (the earliest use of the word we have is in Xenophon, *Anabasis* I, 2, 7 where the royal palace and park of Cyrus, the prince who was satrap (governor) of Phrygia is mentioned). Later it came to mean a formal garden or orchard in a more general sense, but in the New Testament always means "paradise", a place of blessedness above the earth (see Bauer, and Liddell & Scott).

Section 6

pages 29-30
1. This vine. 2.This slave. 3.This work (*or* this deed). 4.This life. 5.This thief. 6.This book. 7.This loaf. 8.This baked fish.
9.This disciple has faith.(*or,* This disciple believes.)
10.Is this wine bad? The prophet says so. (literally, "says this")
11.This man has a fine voice.
12.This disciple is blind.
13.The prophet sees this man.
14.This thief sees the wine.
15.Don't you see this door? I see the door; I don't have the key.
16.Are you sending this man? No (literally, I am not sending (him)); he is blind.
17.I am sending this (one). This woman is sending this man.
18.The prophet says this. 19.This deed is noble.
20.The prophet is writing this book.
21.This man sees the prophet; this woman hears his voice.

Do you believe this?

page 31
1.These men. 2.These men. 3.These (men). 4.These doors. 5.These doors. 6.These deeds. 7.These deeds. 8.These voices. 9.These sheep. 10.These lambs. 11.This farmer. 12.Your testimony.
13.The prophet is sending these disciples. Is he sending these men? Yes.(literally, He is sending these men.)
14.The disciple is baptising these children. Is he baptising these (ones)? He is baptising them.
15.These children are mine.
16.These women accept your testimony. They are friends.
17.Who is taking these loaves and these baked fish?

page 32
1.Of the word. 2.Of the prophet. 3.Of the son. 4.Of Mary. 5.Of life (in general). 6.Of the voice. 7.Of the truth. 8.Of the blind thief. 9.Of the friend(ly man). 10.Of the friend(ly woman). 11.Of the bad deed. 12.Of the teacher himself. 13.Of this bandit. 14.Of the bad baked fish. 15.Of this desert. 16.Of the vine itself.

Section 6

17.I have faith in (or, I believe in) the word of this man.

What is the difference between...?

1.I am sending this slave and	I am sending him.	
2.I see these lads and	I see them.	
3.He is discovering the truth itself	and	he is discovering it.

4.We are writing these books and

we are writing the books themselves.

5.We are disciples of the prophet himself and

We are disciples of this prophet.

6.I believe in this word and

I believe in the word itself.

pages 32-33
1.Who is this man? He is your son.
2.What do these men want? They have no bread.
3.Who believes in (or, Who trusts) the testimony of this prophet?
4.Where are Mary's lambs?
5.Are the farmer's sheep fine?
6.This farmer has fine sheep and fine vines.
7.I do not accept your testimony.
8.We do not see the sea; we hear the sound of it.

page 33
Behold the lamb of God.
This is the son of God.
I am the bread of life.
Do you have faith in (or, Do you believe in) the son of man?
Your word is truth.
His testimony is true.
Rabbi, you are the son of God.
This is the testimony of John.

(a)[1]1.This voice. 2.This friend (masc.). 3.This sheep. 4.Of this prophet.
5.Of this road. 6.Of this deed. 7.The bad friend. 8.The true word. 9.Of

---

[1]These two exercises are in sentence building.   It helps students at this stage
to keep the word pattern of the English as near the Greek word pattern as

Section 6

the loaf. 10.He himself. 11.Of her. 12.Of him (*or*, Of it). 13.We have.
14.You believe. (*or*, You trust) (plural). 15.They hear. 16.The slave
believes. 17.You are looking (*or*, You see). (singular) 18.He/she/it writes.
19.The man has the loaf. 20.The farmer finds the lamb. 21.What do you
want, disciples? 22.We hear (*or*, We are listening to) the voice of the
prophet; he has the key of (i.e., to) eternal life. 23. They do not accept my
testimony. 24. The words of the prophet are not true. 25.We hear the
sound of the sea.

(b)1.The vine. 2.The true vine. 3.We see the thief. 4.They see this thief.
5.We see (or We are looking at) this prophet; we do not hear his words.
6.Of the book. 7.You do not have faith in the words of this book.
8.These slaves. 9.Of this farmer. 10.These slaves belong to this farmer.
(literally, These slaves are of this farmer.)²
11.The voice. 12.The voice of Philip. 13.This is Philip's voice; his words
are true.
14.Mary has these lambs.
15.The friends. 16.The friends of the blind man. 17.The friends of the
blind man are waiting.
18.The teacher himself. 19.The teacher himself says this (literally, says
these things).
page 34
Subject or object?
1.Subject. 2.Object. 3.Object. 4.Object. 5.Object. 6.Subject. 7.Object.
8.Subject. 9.Object. 10.Object. 11.Subject. 12.Object. 13.Object.
14.Subject. 15.Object. 16.Subject or object. 17.Subject or object.
page 35
1.Who has this book? It belongs to the slave. To this slave? Yes.
2.This is the word of the prophet himself. Are the prophet's words true?
Yes (literally, (they are) true); he has the book of life.
3.Are these baked fish good? No (literally, (they are) not good); neither
are these loaves.

---

possible. For instance, it helps to translate βλέπω + object as "I see" rather
than "I look at", and ἀκούω + object as "I hear" rather than "I listen to".
²"I belong" is usually expressed in Greek by εἰμι + a possessive ("I am of ...).

25

4.This man's sons are Andrew and Simon (or, The sons of this man are Simon and Andrew).
5.Does this book belong to Philip? (*or*, Is this Philip's book?)
6.Is this Mary's sheep?

Translation practice involving singular possessives:
1.The son of Philip (or Philip's son). 2.The farmer's friend. 3.Mary's sheep. 4.His voice. 5.The prophet's words. 6.The friends of the truth (*or* The friends of truth). 7.This man's friends (*or* The friends of this man). 8.This woman's friends (*or* The friends of this woman). 9.The friends of Philip and Mary (*or* Philip and Mary's friends).
10.This slave is my friend.
11.The blind man is a friend of this disciple.

More practice involving singular possessives
1.Behold the word of the disciple. 2.Is the word true? Yes (literally, The word of the disciple is true).
3.The prophet's work. 4.The prophet's deeds.
5.Of the deed (*or* Of the work). 6.Of the good deed.
7.I hear (the voice of) the prophet. I hear Mary.
9.Do you hear (*or*, Are you listening to) the prophet?

Optional exercise:
1.οὗτος ὁ γεωργος προβατα καλα ἐχει.
2.ἰδε! οἱ λησται τους ἀμνους αὐτου λαμβανουσιν.
3.τους λογους του προφητου ἀκουομεν, και την μαρτυριαν αὐτου λαμβανομεν.
4.αὐτη ἐστιν ἡ ἐντολη ἡ ἐμη.
5.τις δε ἐστιν οὗτος;
6.οὗτος ἐστιν ὁ υἱος μου.

Additional material.

θεοῦ γὰρ ἐσμεν συνεργοί, θεοῦ γεώργιον, θεοῦ οἰκοδομή ἐστε. (I Corinthians III, 9)

For we are God's co-workers, you are God's farm, God's building.
ὁ συνεργός = the co-worker   τὸ γεώργιον = the farm
ἡ οἰκοδομή = the building

εὐλογεῖτε, πάντα τὰ ἔργα κυρίου, τὸν κύριον·
    ὑμνεῖτε καὶ ὑπερυψοῦτε αὐτὸν εἰς τοὺς αἰῶνας.
εὐλογεῖτε, οὐρανοί, τὸν κύριον·
    ὑμνεῖτε καὶ ὑπερυψοῦτε αὐτὸν εἰς τοὺς αἰῶνας.
εὐλογεῖτε, ἄγγελοι κυρίου, τὸν κύριον,
    ὑμνεῖτε καὶ ὑπερυψοῦτε αὐτὸν εἰς τοὺς αἰῶνας.
εὐλογεῖτε, ὕδατα πάντα τὰ ἐπάνω τοῦ οὐρανοῦ, τὸν κύριον·
    ὑμνεῖτε καὶ ὑπερυψοῦτε αὐτὸν εἰς τοὺς αἰῶνας.
εὐλογεῖτε, ἥλιος καὶ σελήνη, τὸν κύριον·
    ὑμνεῖτε καὶ ὑπερυψοῦτε αὐτὸν εἰς τοὺς αἰῶνας.
εὐλογεῖτε, ἄστρα τοῦ οὐρανοῦ, τὸν κύριον,
    ὑμνεῖτε καὶ ὑπερυψοῦτε αὐτὸν εἰς τοὺς αἰῶνας.

Daniel 3, 57-60 and 62-63 [3]

πάντα (neuter plural) = all   εὐλογεῖτε = praise! (imperative)
ὑμνεῖτε = sing of! (imperative) ὑπερυψοῦτε = exalt![4]
ὁ οὐρανός = heaven   εἰς τοὺς αἰῶνας = for ever
                                                    (literally, into the eternities)
τὰ ὕδατα (plural of τὸ ὕδωρ) = the waters
τὰ ἐπάνω = those on top (followed by "of")
ὁ ἥλιος = the sun   ἡ σελήνη = the moon
τὰ ἄστρα = the stars

Praise, all ye works of the Lord, the Lord
sing (of) Him and exalt Him into the eternities.
Praise, ye heavens, the Lord,
sing (of) him and exalt Him into the eternities
Praise, ye angels of the Lord, the Lord, sing &c.
Praise, all ye waters on top of the heaven, the Lord; sing &c.
Praise, ye sun and moon, the Lord; sing &c
Praise, ye stars of the heaven, the Lord; sing &c.

---

[3] According to the Septuagint version; this song is not in the Masoretic version found in the Old Testament.
[4] 2nd plural present im perative of ὑπερυψόω = I exalt.

page 37
1.He was a prophet. 2.He was not a prophet. 3.He is a prophet. 4.We were disciples. 5.You were a slave.
6.The prophet's slaves were blind.
7.Who was the farmer's friend?
8.Where were you, Ruth and Mary? Where were we? Where were you, friends?
9.Where were the children?
10.Where are the children?
11.Was Nathanael a farmer?
12.Were John and James sons of Zebedee?
pages 38-39
1.From the door. 2.Out of the courtyard (*or* sheepfold). 3.Out of the kingdom of Israel. 4.From the lad himself.(*or*, From his lad.)
5.The disciple is sending this letter from the prophet himself.
6.We hear the words of salvation from this book.
7.They have wine from the vine.
8.This baked fish does not come from the sea (literally, is not out of the sea).
9.Where are you leading these lambs?
10.The farmer is leading the lambs out of the desert.

You are not out of the world.
My kingdom is not out of this world.[1]
And I have other sheep, which are not out of this sheepfold.
page 39
1.of the men. 2.of the letters. 3.of the roads. 4.of the children. 5.of the disciples themselves. 6.of us. 7.of you (plural). 8. from the doors. 9.out of the teacher's books.
page 41
1.We hear Mary now, but we don't see her.
2.I see the prophet, but I don't hear his voice.
3.These are the disciples, but we don't see the prophet.

---

[1]Zerwick & Grosvenor translate: "does not belong to the world".

The anger of God remains upon him.
Salvation comes from the Jews. (literally, is out of the Jews)
You do not have the love of God[2]... and you do not receive me.
You are from (literally, out of) those below, I am from those above.
Is this (man) your son? ... Therefore, how does he now see?
This man is our son.
I am the door of the sheep.
The sheep hear his voice.
But you do not believe; for you are not out of my sheep.
My sheep hear my voice.
There were together Simon Peter and Thomas called Twin and Nathanael
from Cana of Galilee, and the sons of Zebedee, and two others out of his
disciples.

page 42 (Part D)

The same thief	the thief himself
the same door	the door itself
the same lad	the lad himself

page 43

1.The same voice. 2.The same farmer. 3.The same child.
4.They are writing the same book.
5.The lads have the same teacher.
6.The words of the same prophet are true.
7.The thieves see the same sheep.
8.The thief runs away out of the same door.
9.The Lord finds the same blind man.
10.The sheep are from (literally, out of) the same sheepfold.
10.These children say the same things.
11.These brothers have faith in the same prophet.
12.These sisters are from the same village.

---

[2]Barrett (p.269) notes that the genitive may be objective "love towards God" or
subjective "love felt by God", but that the former is more likely.

Section 7

Optional exercise:

1.οὐ πιστευω εἰς τους λογους τουτου του προφητου· ἀληθινοι γαρ οὐκ εισιν.

2.Οὗτοι οἱ ἀρτοι ἐμοι οὐκ εἰσιν· αὐτους οὖν οὐ λαμβανω.

3.ἑπτα οὖν ἀδελφοι ἦσαν.

4.ἀληθως θεοῦ υἱος ἦν οὗτος.

5.το βαπτισμα το[3] ᾽Ιωαννου ἐξ οὐρανου ἦν ἡ ἐξ ἀνθρωπων;

6.ἦν δε ἐγγυς το πασχα των ᾽Ιουδαιων.

Additional material.

εἰ δὲ ὁ ὀφθαλμός σου ὁ δεξιὸς σκανδαλίζει σε, ἔξελε αὐτὸν καὶ βάλε ἀπό σου ... καὶ εἰ ἡ δεξία σου χεὶρ σκανδαλίζει σε, ἔκκοψον αὐτὴν καὶ βάλε ἀπό σου. (Matthew V, 29 and 30)

> *But if your right eye causes you to stumble into sin, pluck it out and throw (it) away from you ... and if your right hand causes you to stumble into sin, cut it off and throw it away from you.*

New words.

ὁ ὀφθαλμός = the eye. δεξιός –ά –όν = right (opp. to left). σκανδαλίζω = I cause to sin [4] ἔξελε = pluck out! (2nd sing. aorist imperative of ἐξαιρέω)[5] βάλε = throw! ἡ χείρ = the hand. ἔκκοψον = cut off!

---

[3]Some mss. omit το.

[4]τὸ σκάνδαλον = the trap (laid for an animal or an enemy); Liddell & Scott cite I Kings XVIII, 21 (Septuagint; I Samuel in the Masoretic Old Testament): καὶ εἶπεν Σαουλ Δώσω αὐτὴν αὐτῷ, καὶ ἔσται αὐτῷ εἰς σκάνδαλον (= I shall give her (sc. Melchol) to him (sc. David), and she shall be for a trap to him.) Liddell & Scott also explain σκανδάληθρον as a stick set upright in a baited trap which causes it to close when knocked over by an animal.

[5]For this imperative and βάλε, see Section 26; for ἔκκοψον, see Section 25.

<u>page 45</u>
(a)1.I take. 2.You find. (plural) 3.They have. 4.We send. 5.You believe.
(singular) 6.The prophet says. 7.The slaves are waiting. 8.The sheep hear.
9.The prophet sees.

(b)1.You are a friend. 2.The work is good. 3.We are blind. 4.The baked
fish were bad. 5.The words are true. 6.You were. (plural)

(c)
1.The farmer finds the lamb.
2.The disciple is writing the book.
3.The bandits are taking the wine.
4.We are sending your friends.
5.The sheep see the thief.
6.Do you (plural) have (any) bread? 7.What do they want? 8.Do you
(plural) see him? 9.Do you (plural) hear this?

(d)
1.The farmer's son has fine lambs.
2.The sheep hear his voice.
3.Do you hear the prophet, disciples?
4.We see the truth of these words.
5.I don't have your wine.
<u>page 46</u>
1.I say[1] to you (singular). 2.He/she/it says to me. 3.You (singular) say to
him. 4.You (plural) say to her. 5.He/she/it says to the farmer. 6.They say
to the slave. 7.We say to the prophet. 8.You (plural) say to the thief.
9.The friends[2] say to her. 10.You (singular) say to the lad. 11.Are you

---

[1] N.B. I say to you = I am telling you, He/she/it says to me = He/she/it is telling me, and
so on.
[2]feminine

(plural) saying to me? 12.I am not saying to you. (singular). 13.The disciples are saying to the blind man's son.

pages 48-49

1.To (towards) the door. 2.In the road. 3.Into the desert. 4.Into the wine. 5.To (towards) the farmers.[3] 6.To (towards) the sheep. 7.Out of the door. 8.Out of the courtyards.

9.The farmer is sending the sheep into the sheepfold.

10.The sheep are remaining in the sheepfold.

11.The thief is taking the sheep out of the sheepfold.

12.The disciples hear the prophet's voice in the desert.

13.The farmer is leading the lamb out of the sheepfold towards the desert.

Jesus' mother says to him, "They don't have wine." (And) Jesus says to her, "What is that to me and you?"

But it was sabbath in (= during) that day.

Are you the[4] teacher of Israel, and don't you know these things?

In beginning[5] was the word, and the word was in the presence of God, and the word was God; this (one) was in beginning in the presence of God.

N.B. εἰς is often used where we should expect ἐν, e.g. John I, 18 ὁ ὢν εἰς τὸν κόλπον τοῦ πατρὸς ("the one who is in the bosom of the father") or Mark X, 10 Καὶ εἰς τὴν οἰκίαν πάλιν οἱ μαθηταὶ περὶ τούτου ἐπηρώτων αὐτόν = and in the house the disciples began to ask him again about this. (v. Bauer, p. 230)

---

[3]One should caution beginners not to expect πρός + accusative always to mean "towards". Sometimes πρός + accusative is used not to mean "towards" but with a verb of saying where we might have expected a dative, e.g. εἶπον οὖν οἱ Ἰουδαῖοι πρὸς ἑαυτούς ("therefore the Jews said to themselves" (John VII, 35).

[4]Barrett notes that the article here expresses emphasis "the well-known teacher"; a similar use of the article is quoted by Moulton (p.142) from Mark VI, 3 οὐχ οὗτος ἐστιν ὁ τέκτων; "Isn't this the well-known carpenter?"

[5]ἐν ἀρχῇ are the first two words of Genesis: ἐν ἀρχῇ ἐποίησεν ὁ θεὸς τὸν οὐρανὸν καὶ τὴν γῆν ("in beginning God made the heaven and the earth"). ἐν ἀρχῇ here means, therefore, "when all things (i.e. the universe) began". (Zerwick & Grosvenor)

Section 8

pages 49-50
1.That teacher. 2.This loaf. 3.The maidservant herself. 4.This maidservant. 5.To (or towards) him. 6.To (or towards) her. 7.To (or towards) us. 8.To (or towards) you. (plural) 9.Towards the door itself. 10.His (or "its"). 11.Hers. 12.That slave's. 13.Of the farmer himself. 14.To (or for) the lad himself. 15.To (or for) her. 16.To (or for) him (or "to it"). 17.To (or for) Mary herself. 18.I am telling this lad (or saying to this lad). 19.I am telling the teacher himself. 20.I am telling that lad. 21.I am telling the prophet himself. 22.I am telling the maidservant herself.

Optional exercise:
1.ὑπαγω προς την θαλασσαν. 2.που ἀγεις ταυτα τα προβατα; εἰς την ἐρημον. 3.ἐν αὐτῳ ζωη ἦν. 4.ἀληθως ἐξ αὐτων εἰ, και[6] γαρ Γαλιλαιος εἰ. 5.οὐκ ἐστιν μαθητης ὑπερ τον διδασκαλον οὐδε δουλος ὑπερ τον κυριον αὐτου.

Additional material
ἰδοὺ ἐγὼ ἀποστέλλω ὑμᾶς ὡς πρόβατα ἐν μέσῳ λύκων.
See, I send you out as sheep in (the) middle of wolves. (Matthew X, 16)
ἀποστέλλω = I send out μέσος = middle (of) ὁ λύκος = the wolf

τί δὲ βλέπεις τὸ κάρφος τὸ ἐν τῷ ὀφθαλμῷ τοῦ ἀδελφοῦ σου, τὴν δὲ ἐν τῷ σῷ ὀφθαλμῷ δοκὸν οὐ κατανοεῖς; ἢ πῶς ἐρεῖς τῷ ἀδελφῷ σου· ἄφες ἐκβαλῶ τὸ κάρφος ἐκ τοῦ ὀφθαλμοῦ σου, καὶ ἰδοὺ ἡ δοκὸς ἐν τῷ ὀφθαλμῷ σου; ὑποκριτά, ἔκβαλε πρῶτον ἐκ τοῦ ὀφθαλμοῦ σου τὴν δοκόν, καὶ τότε διαβλέψεις ἐκβαλεῖν τὸ κάρφος ἐκ τοῦ ὀφθαλμοῦ τοῦ ἀδελφοῦ σου. (Matthew VII, 3-5)
But why do you see the speck in your brother's eye, but the beam of wood in your own eye you do not notice? Or how do you say to your brother, allow (me), let me take the speck out of your eye, and look! the beam in your own eye. Hypocrite, take out first the beam out of your eye, and then you will see clearly to take the speck out of your brother's eye.

---

[6]No. 4 of the optional exercise on p.52 of *An Introduction to New Testament Greek* should read "for indeed you are a Galilaean".

τὸ κάρφος = the speck (for neuter –ος nouns, see section 23B) ὁ ὀφθαλμός = the eye ἡ δοκός = the beam (of wood) κατανοέω = I notice ἤ = or ἐρεῖς = you will say (used as future of λέγω) ἄφες = allow! ἐκβαλῶ = let me take out (aorist subjunctive of ἐκβάλλω; see section 26) ὑποκριτά is vocative from ὁ ὑποκριτής = hypocrite ἔκβαλε = take out! (aorist imperative of ἐκβάλλω; see section 26) διαβλέπω = I see clearly (for διαβλέψεις, future, see section 23) ἐκβαλεῖν = to take out (aorist infinitive of ἐκβάλλω; see section 26)

<u>page 53</u>
1.This vine. 2.That teacher. 3.That deed (or work). 4.During that day.
5.These lambs. 6.Into this courtyard.
7.The prophet is sending these disciples into the desert.
8.What do you want, disciples? 9.We want everlasting life.
10.The other thief. 11.Do you hear? (plural) 12.Does he/she/it find?
13.He/she/it finds the truth. 14.The other thief hears (listens to) the words
of the prophet, and discovers the truth.
15.What are you saying? (plural) 16.Now I know.[1]
17.This is God's day.
18.This is the fine shepherd and these are his sheep.
19.Is this your son? Yes. (literally, It is.)
20.Do you see the other door? Yes. (literally, I see (it).)
21.These loaves are mine.
22.My words are true.
<u>pages 54-55</u>
He says to them.
Jesus says to them.
Truly, truly, I say to you.
After this he says to them: "Our friend Lazarus has fallen asleep."
He says to them, "<u>I</u> am (he)."[2]
And he says to them, "Behold the man."
Jesus says to her, "Mary."
Therefore they say to the blind man again, "What do <u>you</u> say about him?"
There is in Jerusalem near the sheep gate a pool, which is called in Hebrew
Bethesda.
He says to his disciples.

---

[1]i.e., I have only learned it just now.

[2]Barrett (p.342), in his note on John VIII, 24 cautions against hastily concluding that the use of ἐγώ εἰμι is intended (as the equivalent of the Hebrew *'ani hu*) to equate Jesus with the supreme God of the Old Testament. Zerwick & Grosvenor refer to Mark XIII, 6, where Jesus predicts that others who claim falsely to be the Messiah will say ἐγώ εἰμι.

Section 9

page 56
1.Who says these things?[3] What does Nicodemus say?
2.Why does he say these things? (Why does he say that?)
3.Why are you waiting, friends? Do you want bread?
4.Who knows these things? (Who knows that?)
5.Where is the wine?
6.How do you say these things (that) in Hebrew?

I know where I came from and where I am going away to.
And he says to Jesus, "Whence are you?" ("Where do you come from?")
Through what kind of ... deed are you stoning me?
How much do you owe to my lord?

pages 57-58
1.Don't you know this? 2.You aren't saying that, are you?
3.Isn't this Nathanael?
4.You aren't going away to the desert again, are you? (Surely you aren't going away to the desert again?)
5.Surely the deeds of these men aren't wicked, are they?
6.Where are you leading these sheep? I'm leading them from the temple through the sheep gate towards the pool in Bethesda.
7.Why don't you say that to the doorkeeper?
8.What kind of book is this? The words of the prophets are in it.
9.How do you know that? Because on every occasion the disciples tell us the truth.
10.Why don't you understand these words? Because the disciple is writing them in Hebrew.
11.Don't you see the doorkeeper and the maidservant? They are chasing the thieves out of the courtyard.
12.Where are the other disciples? They are waiting in the headquarters, but the children are in the temple.

He says to him, "Lord, who is it?"
  Simon Peter says to him, Lord, where are you going away to?"[4]

---

[3] See footnote 10, p.55 of *An Introduction to New Testament Greek*.

[4] "Whither?" is ποῖ in Classical Greek, but in the New Testament always ποῦ.

Section 9

Therefore the maidservant (who was) the doorkeeper says to Peter,"Surely you aren't one of this man's disciples too, are you?"
Therefore they lead Jesus from Caiaphas to the official residence.
After that, Jesus finds him in the temple.
But I, because I tell the truth, you don't believe me.
And I am no longer in the world, and these men are in the world.
For their deeds were wicked.

Optional exercise:
1.ὁ διδασκαλος παντοτε ταυτα τοις των γεωργων υἱοις λεγει. 2.τους κακους μαθητας τοις ἐργοις (αὐτῶν) γινωσκομεν. 3.πως γινωσκετε τι θελομεν; 4.οὐχι συ εἰ ὁ χριστος; 5.τι ἐτι σκυλλεις τον διδασκαλον; 6.ὁ δε λεγει αὐτοις, ποσους ἀρτους ἐχετε;

Additional material

ἴδετε, ἴδετε[5] ὅτι ἐγώ εἰμι,
καὶ οὐκ ἐστιν θεὸς πλὴν ἐμοῦ. (Deuteronomy XXXII, 39) (Septuagint)
See! See that I am and there is no god except me.
ἴδετε is 2nd plural aorist imperative from ὁράω (section 26) and means "see!" For πλήν, see the appendix to section 8.

δόξα ἐν ὑψίστοις θεῷ
καὶ ἐπὶ γῆς εἰρήνη
ἐν ἀνθρώποις εὐδοκίας   (Luke II, 14)
Glory in the highest things to God / and on earth peace / among men of his approval.
ἡ δόξα = glory ἡ γῆ = land, earth (for other notes, see the reader, *An Introduction to New Testament Greek*, p.277).[6]

---

[5]Plural imperative, "behold!"
[6]The angels' song refers to no. 18 of the apocryphal Psalms of Solomon, verse 10:
Μέγας ἡμῶν ὁ θεὸς καὶ ἔνδοξος ἐν ὑψίστοις κατοικῶν ... (= Great is our God and glorious, dwelling in the highest...)

Section 10

page 59
1.You are. (plural) 2,.You hear. (singular) 3.They see. 4.Are they writing? 5.We know. 6.You are taking. (plural) 7.Do I believe? 8.I was. 9.He/she/it is going away. 10.Does he/she/it send?

1.It is the Lord. 2.The prophets are writing. 3.The maidservant is beautiful. 4.The lads are waiting. 5.Are you waiting, doorkeepers? 6.They (these women) are waiting.

1.We are writing a fine book. 2.These prophets are evil; they do not tell the truth. 3.The bandit is taking the sheep and going away. 4.The farmer does not see him, for he is blind.

1.We do not accept your testimony; but we listen to the voice of the teacher and we believe him. 2.The disciples of this prophet do not have another teacher. 3.But the maidservant's words are true.

1.After that, what do you want? 2.What is the prophet saying to the disciples? We do not hear. 3.He is leading them into the desert, but they do not trust (have faith in) his words.
4.Where are you leading these sheep? What is it to you? I am leading my lambs towards the farmer's sheepfold.
5.Just now, we see bandits in this sheepfold.
6.This isn't true, is it? Where are they from? We don't know that.
page 60
1.To baptise. 2.To believe. 3.To hear. 4.To take. 5.To wait. 6.To want. 7.To know.
8.This prophet is telling the truth, but the disciples no longer want to hear it.
9.The farmer does not see the thieves yet; but they are still waiting in the sheepfold, for they want to take the sheep.
10.Don't the lads want to find the teacher?

Section 10

I still have many things to say to you.[1]
You[2] do not want to come to me.
You aren't a Galilaean also, are you?
You[3] don't want to go away too, do you?
pages 62-63
There was Andrew, Simon Peter's brother, one of the two *who had heard from John and started to follow him.* He (this man) first finds his own brother and says to him, "We have found the Messiah."
But there were six stone water-jars there...holding two or three measures each.
You say that in Jerusalem is the place where it is necessary to worship.
We have one father, God.
I and the father are one thing.
One of his disciples, Andrew, Simon Peter's brother, says to him, "There is one lad here who has five loaves made of barley flour and two baked fish; but what is that into so many?"
page 64
1.With Mary. 2.With Nicodemus. 3.After the work. 4.With the slave.
5.With the friends. 6.Of the lad. 7.With these men (or women). 8.After that.
9.The maidservant is going away with her own friends.
10.After these words the disciples are going away into the temple.
11.This man was with the prophet.
12.After the first day the farmers don't have (any) wine.
13.After that, the doorkeeper says "What do you want?"

But Thomas, one of the twelve, the one called Didymus, was not with them. And after eight days the disciples were inside again and Thomas with them. Therefore Jesus said to the twelve, "You don't want to go away too, do you?"

Optional exercise:
1.οἱ λογοι ἑνος των προφητων ἐν ταυτῃ τῃ βιβλῳ εἰσιν.

---

[1]plural
[2]plural
[3]plural

39

Section 10

2. οὐ θελεις[4] την άληθειαν γινωσκειν.

3. τις τουτων των τριων πλησιον δοκει σοι;[5]

4. και συν αὐτῷ σταυρουσιν δυο λῃστας, ἑνα ἐκ δεξιων και ἑνα ἐξ εὐωνυμων αὐτου.

5. ἐρχεται μια των παιδισκων.

6. και ιδου, δυο ἐξ αὐτων ἐν αὐτῃ τῃ ἡμερᾳ ἡσαν πορευομενοι εἰς κωμην.

Additional material

οὐδεὶς δύναται δυσὶ κυρίοις δουλεύειν· ἢ γὰρ τὸν ἕνα μισήσει καὶ τὸν ἕτερον ἀγαπήσει, ἢ ἑνὸς ἀνθέξεται καὶ τοῦ ἑτέρου καταφρονήσει. οὐ δύνασθε θεῷ δουλεύειν καὶ μαμωνᾷ.

(Matthew VI, 24)

No one is able to be a slave to two lords; for either he will hate the one and love (value) the other, or he will be a devotee of one and he will be scornful of the other. You are not able to be a slave to God and mammon.

οὐδείς = no one (literally, "and not one") δύναται = is able (section 17) δουλεύω = I am a slave (*or* I am a servant) ἢ ... ἢ ... = either ... or ... μισήσει = he will hate (3rd person singular future active of μισέω, section 23) ὁ ἕτερος = the other (of two, the alternative) ἀγαπήσει = he will love (i.e., value) (3rd person singular future active of ἀγαπάω)[6] ἀνθέξεται is 3rd person singular future middle of ἀντέχω (+ genitive) = I cling to, am a devotee of (section 24) καταφρονήσει is 3rd person singular future active of καταφρονέω (section 23) and means "will look down (on)", i.e. "will be scornful (of)" δύνασθε is 2nd person plural present of δύναμαι (section 17) Μαμωνᾷ is the dative singular of ὁ Μαμωνᾶς, from the Aramaic *Mam²n* , meaning "wealth" (see Bauer, p.490).

---

[4] or θελετε.

[5] v. 36 is in full τίς τούτων τῶν τρίων πλησίον δοκεῖ σοι γεγονέναι τοῦ ἐμπεσόντος εἰς τοὺς λῃστάς; (= who of these three seems to you to have become neighbour of the (man) having fallen among thieves?). γεγονέναι is the perfect infinitive active of γίνομαι and ἐμπεσόντος is the genitive singular masculine of the aorist participle active of ἐμπίπτω, from ἐνέπεσον, strong aorist. For these forms, see sections 26 and 29 of *An Introduction to New Testament Greek*, pp. 208 and 253 respectively. (πλησίον is an adverb, and so is indeclinable.)

[6] See *An Introduction to New Testament Greek*, p.136

40

Section 11

page 71
1.You say. (singular) 2.What do you say? (singular) 3.He/she/it says.
4.You baptise. (singular) 5.You believe. (plural) 6.They don't believe.
7.We take. 8.You find. (singular) 9.Don't you know? (plural) 10. He
doesn't see, does he? (*or* She doesn't see, does she?) 11.I haven't (any)
bread. 12.Don't you (singular) have wine? 13.He/she is writing a book.
14.The doorkeeper is waiting. 15.The doorkeeper is waiting. 16.I hear his
voice. 17.Do you hear the voice of the prophet? 18.The farmer is leading
the lamb to the temple after the prophet.

page 72
1.Do they ask?[1] 2.The slave is not asking this. 3.What are you doing?
(plural) 4.Who is doing that?[2] 5.I am showing this to you.[3] 6.What are
you (singular) showing to me?

pages 73-74
1.You honour. (plural) 2.He/she/it seeks. 3.We are walking about. 4.You
are helping. (*or* You help.) (plural) 5.They are watching. 6.You are
speaking. (singular) 7.He/she/it is calling. 8.You are filling. (singular)
9.You are setting free. (plural) 10.We are testifying. 11.You are blowing.
(plural) 12.He/she/it is making (something) smaller. 13.You are not
revealing. (singular) 14.Are you searching? (singular) 15.The prophet is
speaking. 16.What do you think? (singular) 17.The slave is doing a fine
job. 18.How do they worship? 19.We are seeking him. 20.Who is walking
about in the courtyard? 21.The thief is watching the wine. 22.Where are
you going away to? (plural) 23.The maidservant is asking the teacher this.
24.Who are you? she asks. (*or* he asks) 25.The lads respect the teacher.
26.Why are you (singular) following me?

The wind (spirit)[4] blows where it wishes, and you hear the sound of it.

---

[1]i.e. do they enquire? αἰτέω tends to be used for "I ask" meaning "I request".
[2]p.55, footnote 10.
[3]σοί (singular pronoun, with accent) implies emphasis.
[4]Both Bauer and Zerwick and Grosvenor translate τὸ πνεῦμα as "wind" here, but
Zerwick and Grosvenor point out that in verse 6 it means "spirit". Barrett (*The Gospel
according to St. John* pp.210-211) explains that the Hebrew word "ruah" has the same

Section 11

Therefore what sign[5] are you making?

You search the scriptures because you expect[6] in them to have eternal life.

My sheep hear my voice, and I know them, and they follow me.

Yet a little (while), and the world no longer perceives me.

Why[7] do you ask me?

Therefore Pilate says to him, "Do you not speak to me?"

You[8] call me "teacher" and "Lord", and you say well, for I am.

page 75

1.to speak. 2.to testify. 3.to honour. 4.to help. 5.to watch, notice *or* perceive. 6.to make smaller. 7.to call. 8.to seek. 9.to search. 10.to worship. 11.to ask (enquire). 12.to fill. 13.to walk about. 14.to set free. 15.to think *or* to seem. 16.to reveal. 17.to blow.

18.The farmer wants us to search the desert, for he is seeking the lamb.

19.The prophet wants to speak to the disciples; therefore he is calling them.

20.You don't want to set the bandit free, do you? (*or* Surely you don't want to set the bandit free, do you?)

21.We must not make this coat smaller. For it is already small.

What sign do you show us, that[9] you do these things?

No one can do these signs (miracles) which you do.

The world cannot hate you,[10] but it hates me, because I testify about it that its deeds are wicked.

They say the scriptures to be true.[11]

I want to be your friend.

---

double meaning, which cannot be reproduced in English, and that St. John has both meanings in mind here.

[5]τὸ σημεῖον is the word used in John for the miracles of Jesus. δυνάμεις, "powers" is often used for "miracles" in Matthew, Luke, Acts and the Epistles of Paul.

[6]literally, you think in them to have eternal life, i.e. you suppose that in them you have eternal life.

[7]In this context, τί stands for διὰ τί.

[8]plural

[9]"in regard to the fact that" (Moulton, *A treatise on the Grammar of New Testament Greek*, p.557, who says that ὅτι points to some existing fact, something that lies before us).

[10]plural

[11]i.e. They say that the scriptures are true.

42

Section 11

It is a wicked thing to be a bandit.
page 76
Optional exercise:
1.τι ζητειτε, Ρουθ και Μαρια;   τον γεωργον ὠφελουμεν.   ἡμας τους
ἀμνους αὑτου εὑρισκειν θελει.
2.ὁ προφητης θελει την ἀληθειαν τοις μαθηταις δηλουν.[12]
3.τις ἐστιν οὑτος ὁς λαλει βλασφημιας;
4.τι ποιειτε τουτο;
5.τι ἡ γενεα αὑτη ζητει σημειον;
6.τι με ἐρωτᾳς περι του ἀγαθου;

Additional material
ὁ ἀγαθὸς ἄνθρωπος ἐκ τοῦ ἀγαθοῦ θησαυροῦ τῆς καρδίας προφέρει
τὸ ἀγαθόν, καὶ ὁ πονηρὸς ἐκ τοῦ πονηροῦ προφέρει τὸ πονηρόν.[13] ...
τί δέ με καλεῖτε κύριε, κύριε καὶ οὐ ποιεῖτε ἃ λέγω; (Luke VI, 45-46)

The good man out of the storehouse of his heart brings forth   *the good,*
and the wicked man out of the wicked brings forth the wicked. ... Why do
you call me Lord, Lord and don't do what I say?

New words: ἀγαθός ἀγαθή ἀγαθόν = good ὁ θησαυρός = treasure,
storehouse προφέρω = I bring forth ἃ = which (things) (see section 14)

---

[12]or δεικνυειν or φανερουν.
[13]The words omitted ἐκ γὰρ τοῦ περισσεύματος καρδίας λαλεῖ τὸ στόμα
αὑτοῦ (*for out of the abundance of the heart speaks his mouth*) anticipate section 12
(τοῦ περισσεύματος = of the abundance (genitive of τὸ περίσσευμα) and τὸ
στόμα (also declined like τὸ ὄνομα) = the mouth).

43

page 77
1.one (masc.) one (fem.) one (neut.) 2.One word. One kingdom. One sheep. One road. One child. 3.There is one slave in the courtyard.
4.There is one door in the temple.
5.The thief is taking one lamb.
6.The teacher has one child.
7.The prophets have one maidservant.
8.This is the work of one man.
9.The doorkeeper is saying this to one of the disciples.

page 78
1.We say this to nobody. 2.Nobody is calling. 3.No maidservant is listening. 4.We are doing nothing. 5.We are sending nobody. 6.The slave doesn't listen to anybody. 7.Nobody knows this. 8.We see nothing here.
9.He says nothing to us. 10.The book doesn't belong to anybody, *or*, It is nobody's book. (literally, The book is of nobody.) 11.They show this to nobody *or* They don't show this to anybody.

page 79
1.I am looking for my father. 2.Are you (plural) looking for your mother?
3.They don't hear their father's voice. 4.We are showing the book to (our) mother. 5.Do you say nothing to your father? *or* Don't you say anything to your father?

pages 81-82
(a)
1.What is the name of this slave?
2.This place has no name. (This place doesn't have a name.)
3.The mother's name is Mary.
4.The farmer is speaking to the lad's father.
5.I don't know the name of this lad.
6.In our own country (our fatherland) nobody believes in this prophet.
7.We know him by name.
8.This is (my) mother's house.
9.They don't say their father's name to anybody. (They say their father's name to no one.)

(b) Do not make my father's house a house of trade.[1]
A prophet in his own country does not have honour.
Where is your father?
Just as the father knows me, I also know the father.
The deeds which I do in my father's name, these testify about me; but you do not believe; for you are not out of[2] my sheep. My sheep hear my voice and I know them and they follow me.

1.Subject. 2.Object. 3.Possessive. 4.Indirect object. 5.Object. 6.Object. 7.Possessive. 8.Indirect object. 9.Object. 10.Subject. 11.Ambiguous: subject or object. 12.Possessive. 13.Indirect object.

1.The name.
The maidservant is asking the name of the disciple.
2.In the fatherland.
In your own country, what is your name? (What name do you have?)
3.Of the father.
I have my father's name.
4.The house of the father.
This is the door of your father's house.
5.By this name.
We know him by this name.
6.I notice my father in the market. He is talking to my mother. What are they looking for?

Optional exercise:
1.ὁ πατηρ (μου) τη μητρι (μου) ἐκ του ἐμποριου ἀκολουθει.[3]
2.οὐδεις γινωσκει το ὀνομα της του προφητου πατριδος.
3.οὐκ ἀκουετε την του ἀνεμου φωνην, τεκνα;
4.οὐδεμια παιδισκη ἠν ἐν τῳ του ποιμενος οἰκῳ.

---

[1]Bauer regards ἐμπορίου as an "epexegetic" genitive; this would make the literal translation of οἰκος ἐμπορίου "a house of a market house", i.e., "a house that is or consists of a market house".
[2]i.e. "from among". We might say "you do not come from my flock".
[3]Or ὁ ἐμος πατηρ τη ἐμη μητρι ἐκ του ἐμποριου ἀκολουθει.

5.καὶ ἰδοὺ ἄνθρωπος ἦν ἐν Ἰερουσαλημ ᾧ ὄνομα[4] Συμεων.
6.καὶ λεγουσιν αὐτῷ· ἰδοὺ ἡ μητηρ σου καὶ οἱ ἀδελφοι σου καὶ αἱ ἀδελφαι σου ἔξω ζητουσιν σε.

Additional material

Ναβουχοδονοσορ ὁ βασιλεὺς εἶπεν αὐτοῖς Διὰ τί, Σεδραχ, Μισαχ, Αβεδναγω, τοῖς θεοῖς μου οὐ λατρεύετε καὶ τῇ εἰκόνι τῇ χρυσῇ, ἥν ἔστησα, οὐ προσκυνεῖτε; ... εἰ δὲ μή γε, γινώσκετε ὅτι ἐμβλήσεσθε εἰς τὴν κάμινον τοῦ πυρὸς τὴν καιομένην.

(Daniel III, 14 & 15) (Septuagint).

Nebuchadnezzar the king said to them, "Why, Shedrach, Mesach, Abednego, do you not do service to my gods and to the golden image, which I have put up, do you not bow down? ... But if (you do) not, indeed, you know that you will be thrown into the burning furnace of fire."

βασιλεύς = king εἶπεν = said λατρεύω (+ dat) = I do service to ἡ εἰκών = the image χρυσους χρυσῇ χρυσοῦν = golden [5] ἥν = which (fem. sing. acc.) ἔστησα = I (have) set up (1st sing. weak aorist active of ἵστημι (*Introd. NT Gk.*, p.332)) ἐμβλήσεσθε (2nd plu future passive of ἐμβάλλω) = you will be thrown ἡ κάμινος = the furnace τὸ πῦρ (τοῦ πυρός) = the fire καιόμενος = burning.

ὁ πατήρ and ἡ μήτηρ, although very common and easy to remember, are, of course, slightly irregular because they drop ε in the genitive and dative singular. In practice, this gives little trouble in learning to read Greek, though it would be more important in learning to write Greek. However, if it is desired to give pattern nouns that are completely regular, ποιμήν could be used as an example of masculines, and πατρίς of feminines, as follows:

---

[4]Luke omits ἦν.
[5]Contracted from χρύσεος, χρύσεα, χρύσεον.

SUBJECT (nominative)	ὁ ποιμήν = the shepherd
(OBJECT) (accusative)	τὸν ποιμένα = the shepherd
(POSSESSIVE) (genitive)	τοῦ ποιμένος = of the shepherd
INDIRECT OBJECT (dative)	τῷ ποιμένι = to/for the shepherd

SUBJECT (nominative)	ἡ πατρίς = the fatherland
OBJECT (accusative)	τὴν πατρίδα = the fatherland
POSSESSIVE (genitive)	τῆς πατρίδος = of the fatherland
INDIRECT OBJECT (dative)	τῇ πατρίδι = to/for/by the fatherland

page 83

1. The fatherland. (nominative) 2.Of the mother. 3.By the name.
4.Towards the fatherland.
5.The son is writing his mother's name in the book.
6.What is the doorkeeper's name?

page 84

1.After this, the fathers are unwilling to wait.
2.The maidservants want to find their mothers.
3.The lads do not see their fathers.
4.The names of the brothers are Andrew and Simon.
5.Who is asking the brothers' names?
6.We know the sisters by their names.
7.The maidservants are going away to their fathers' houses.
8.Nobody sees the wind. But we hear its sound.
9.The disciple does the work just as the prophet shows (him).
10.Your fathers are walking about in the desert.

page 85

1.For one day. 2.For two days. 3.Within two days. 4.Within one day.
5.On the second day.
6.We are staying in Jerusalem for one day.
7.Within three days it was the festival of the Jews.
8.On the third day of the festival the disciples walk about in the desert.

page 86 *(top)*

1.He/she says nothing. 2.Everyone knows this. (literally, There's no one who doesn't know this.) 3.The disciples hate no one. 4.Everyone hears the prophet. (literally, There's no one who doesn't hear the prophet.) 5.The true prophet judges no one according to the flesh.

pages 86-88

Third, first, second, third, second, first, first, second.

You say, "If we were in the days of our fathers, we would not be their accomplices in the blood of the prophets."
Still for a little while I am with you.
After that was a festival of the Jews.

You are doing the deeds of your father.
You judge according to the flesh, I do not judge anybody.
The spirit is the life-giving thing, the flesh does not help at all.
On the next day, he sees Jesus coming towards him, and he says, "Behold the lamb of God."
And on the third day a wedding happened in Cana in[1] Galilee and the mother of Jesus was there.

You are from your father the devil, and you want to perform the desires of your father. He[2] was a man-slayer from the beginning[3] ... because truth is not in him ... Who from among you convicts me concerning sin? If I am speaking the truth, why do you not believe me? The man who comes from God[4] hears the words of God; this is the reason you don't listen to me, that you don't come from God.

Optional exercises
1.Object. 2.Possessive. 3.Possessive. 4.Object. (accusative plural) 5.Indirect object. 6.Object. 7.Indirect object. 8.Subject. 9.Object. 10.Indirect object. 11.Possessive. 12.Possessive. 13.Subject. 14.Indirect object.

1.Why are you (singular) walking about in the desert?
2.I am going away to my own country.
3.The sheep are in this sheepfold. They are staying there for three days.
4.On the first day of the festival, the prophet leads us out of the temple.
5.The slave is filling the water pots, but no one wants the wine.
6.About this saying, every one seeks the truth. (literally, no one does not seek the truth)

---

[1]literally, "of Galilee", i.e., part of Galilee.
[2]literally, "That one..."
[3]A reference to the fact that Satan robbed Adam of immortality. "Adam" is a Hebrew word for "man". The Septuagint version of Genesis I begins ἐν ἀρχῇ ("In the beginning...").
[4]literally, "is out of God".

Section 13

1. αἱ των τεκνων μητερες εἰσιν ὧδε.
2. μετα των ποιμενων⁵ τρεις ἡμερας μενομεν.
3. οὐδεν οὐ ποιουσιν οἱ γεωργοι τῃ πρωτῃ ἡμερᾳ της ἑορτης.
4. των δε δωδεκα ἀποστολων τα ὀνοματα ἐστιν ταυτα.
5. εἰ οὖν Δαυιδ καλει αὐτον κυριον, πως υἱος αὐτου ἐστιν;
6. ὑμων δε μακαριοι οἱ ὀφθαλμοι ὁτι βλεπουσιν και τα ὦτα ὑμων ὁτι ἀκουουσιν.⁶

Additional material.

οὐκ ἐπ' ἀρτῳ μόνῳ ζήσεται ὁ ἄνθρωπος, ἀλλ' ἐπὶ πάντι ῥήματι τῷ ἐκπορευομένῳ διὰ στόματος θεοῦ ζήσεται ὁ ἄνθρωπος.
Deuteronomy VIII, 3 (Septuagint)
Not on bread alone shall man live, but on every word proceeding out through the mouth of God shall man live.
ζήσεται (3rd singular future middle of ζάω (section 24, p.180) = shall live πάντι (dat. neut. sing. of πᾶς, section 15) = every ἐκπορευομένῳ (dat. neut. sing. of present participle of ἐκπορεύομαι (sections 17 and 18) = proceeding forth τὸ στόμα, τοῦ στόματος = the mouth.

καὶ ποιμένες ἦσαν ἐν τῇ χώρᾳ τῇ αὐτῇ ἀγραυλοῦντες καὶ φυλάσσοντες φυλακὰς τῆς νυκτὸς ἐπὶ τὴν ποίμνην αὐτῶν.
(Luke II, 8)
And shepherds were in the same country living in the fields and keeping watch (literally, keeping turns at picket duty) during the night over their flock.
ἡ χώρα = the country For τῇ αὐτῇ see section 7, p.42. ἀγραυλέω = I live out of doors (ἀγραυλοῦντες and φυλάσσοντες are nom. masc. plu of present participles, for which see section 16) φυλάσσω = I guard ἡ φυλακή = guard duty (this is an internal accusative, literally "guarding guard duties") ἡ νύξ, τῆς νυκτός = the night (the genitive indicates time "within which") ἡ ποίμνη = the flock.

(This passage is included in the reader, p. 276.)

---

⁵Or συν τοις ποιμεσιν.
⁶The rule that a neuter plural subject is qualified by a singular verb is not invariable.

Section 14

page 89
1.For one day 2.On the third day 3. To/for the mother 4.To/for the fathers 5.Of the names 6.Of the blood 7.By the wind/spirit 8.In the flesh 9.On the next day 10.The sayings.

11.The son of the teacher helps no one.

12.In the sayings of this prophet they find the truth.

13.You judge this according to the flesh.

page 90[1]
1.Trust! (singular) 2.Go away! (plural) 3.Hear! (*or* listen!) (plural) 4.Let him/her say 5.Let them take (*or* receive) 6.Stay here! (plural) 7.Let him/her/it stay there. 8.Don't look! (singular) 9.Don't believe! (plural) 10.Let him/her not know. 11.Let them not hear.

12.Do not say this to the disciples. Say nothing.

13.Let the shepherds not find the sheep.

14.Let no one want to have honour in his own fatherland.

15.Be pure, disciples.

16.Do not be a friend of this world, my son.

page 91
1.Do we know? 2.You do not know. 3.The slave knows. 4.They know this. 5.You don't know, do you?

6.The son of Bartholomew knows this.

7.Surely the friends of the Pharisees don't know this, do they?

8.Who knows the names of the farmer's children?

9.Who knows the truth of this word? Nobody knows (that).

page 93
(a)1.This is the sheep which I am looking for.

2.This is the servant girl who follows the prophet.

---

[1]Aorist imperatives are introduced on p.201 of *An Introduction to New Testament Greek* (section 25). It is explained there that the aorist imperative is normally used for a single request or instruction, and that the present imperative tends to be used for general or continuing requests and instructions. Moulton, *A Treatise on the Grammar of NT Greek*, p.395, says that the distinction between the present and aorist imperatives is generally observed in the New Testament, though of course it depends on the feeling of the writer, and the aorist is the more urgent. He notes that a few imperatives, such as φέρε, "fetch (it)!", are found only in the present, and a few only in the aorist.

3.This is the prophet whom the servant girl follows.
4.The farmer is the man whom I want to see.
5.You are the man whose father I know.
6.These are the writings in which we find the truth.
7.Do not trust the man who has bad friends.
8.The lad has the fish which you want.
9.These are the water jars which they fill with wine.

(b)Go away (in)to your house.
While you have the light, trust in the light.
You believe in God, trust also in me. *(indicative followed by imperative)*
or Trust in God, trust also in me. *(both verbs imperative)*
He who has ears to hear, let him hear.
Beware of the yeast of the Pharisees, and the yeast of Herod.
Go away behind me, Satan.
Truly, truly I say to you that we speak what we know and we testify to what we have seen, and you do not receive our testimony.
Is not this man Jesus the son of Joseph, whose father and mother we know?
Don't you know that the friendship of the world is enmity towards[2] God?
But let your word "yes" be "yes" and your "no" "no"; (going) beyond these is of the evil one.
If anyone does not love the Lord, let him be something accursed.
page 94
Do not store up for yourselves treasures on the earth, where moth and corrosion make them disappear and thieves break in and steal; but store up for yourselves treasures in heaven, where neither moth nor corrosion make them disappear, and where thieves do not break in nor steal; for where your treasure is, there your heart will also be.
page 95
When therefore they had eaten breakfast Jesus says to Simon Peter, Simon, (son) of John, do you love me more than these (men)? He says to him, "Yes, Lord, you know that I love you." Jesus says to him, "Feed my little lambs." Jesus says to him again for a second time, "Simon, son of John, do

---

[2]τοῦ θεοῦ is an objective genitive, like "hatred of God", i.e. "hatred felt towards God."

you delight in (love) me?" He says to him, "Yes, Lord, you know that I love you." He says to him, "Feed my sheep." He says to him the third time, "Simon, son of John, do you love me?" Peter was grieved because Jesus said to him for the third time, "Simon, son of John, do you love me?" and he says to him, "Lord, you know all things, you know that I love you." He says to him, "Feed my sheep."

Optional exercise:
1.τις ἐστιν το παιδαριον ᾧ ὁ ποιμην την ὁδον δηλοι;[3]
2.Μηδεις ταυτα λεγετω.
3.ὑμεις ἐστε το φως του κοσμου.
4.μακαριοι[4] οἱ πτωχοι τῳ πνευματι, ὁτι αὐτων ἐστιν ἡ βασιλεια των οὐρανων.
5.τοτε οἱ ἐν τῃ Ἰουδαιᾳ φευγετωσαν.
6.ἰσθι εὐνοων τῳ ἀντιδικῳ σου.

---

[3]or δεικνυει or φανεροι.
[4]For the word order, see *An Introduction to New Testament Greek,* p.11 (section3).

Section 15

pages 97-98
1.Examine! (singular) 2.Diminish! (singular) 3.Follow me! (singular) 4.Seek! (plural) 5.Ask! (plural) 6.Do not walk about! (plural) 7.Don't look! (plural) 8.Don't watch! (plural) 9.Let him/her/it help. 10.Let them love 11.Let him/her/it fill 12.Let them ask 13.Let him/her/it not speak 14.Let them not testify.

15.Let them not set the slaves of the temple free.[1]

16.Take me to Jerusalem, father; for I want to see the temple.

17.Ask the doorkeeper, servant girls.

18.Do not speak to the bad disciples, friends.

page 99
1.They put. 2.He/she /it does not give. 3.He/she/it does not put. 4.What are they giving?

5.Mothers give names to their children.[2]

6.The shepherd puts the lambs in the fold.

7.Give this lamb to your father, Joseph.

8.Put the water pot here, slave. We do not give wine to the lads.[3]

9.Why do you not give us a sign, prophet?

10.We want to give you these things.

11.Let them not place this here.

page 100
1.Every man. 2.Every sound (*or* voice). 3.Every baked fish. 4.Of every shepherd. 5.To every maidservant. 6.By every deed. 7.By every name. 8.The whole of Judaea. 9.In the whole sheepfold/courtyard. 10.Of all the fathers. 11.To/for all the sisters.

pages 101-102
(a)1.Do not follow these men; everything that they do is evil.

2.All who judge according to the flesh are in error.

3.He shows to us all the glory of this kingdom.

---

[1]If it were "let them not set the slaves free from the temple", "from" would normally be expressed by ἀπό (see Bauer, p251).

[2]*or*, The mothers are giving names to the children.

[3]or "we do not give wine to lads (in general)", taking τὰ παιδάρια to mean "lads in general" or "the class of beings which are lads".

5 4

4.He gives bread and wine to all the shepherds.

(b) She told him the whole truth.

The head steward calls the bridegroom and says to him "Every man first puts out the good wine."

My father gives you the true bread from heaven.

I am the good shepherd. The good shepherd lays down his life on behalf of the sheep.

Just as my father knows me, I also know the father and I lay down my life on behalf of the sheep.

For this reason the father loves[4] me because I lay down my life ... no one takes it away from me, but I put it down from myself (i.e., of my own accord).

My sheep hear my voice and I know them, and they follow me, and I give eternal life to them.

For the father loves the son and shows him everything which he himself does.

(The devil) shows him all the kingdoms of the world and their glory.

Optional exercise:

1.ἐν τῃ ἐρημῳ θησαυρον ζητειτε· τους προφητας[5] περι της ἀληθειας ἐρωτατε.[6]

2.δηλουτωσαν[7] οἱ μαθηται την ὁδον πασιν τοις τυφλοις.

3.πασαις ταις παιδισκαις μη ἀκολουθει·[8] παντα οὐ γινωσκουσιν.[9]

4.τιμα τον πατερα και την μητερα.

5.λεγει αὐτοις· θαρσειτε, ἐγω εἰμι.

6.κατα δε τα ἐργα αὐτων μη ποιειτε· λεγουσιν γαρ και οὐ ποιουσιν.

---

[4]delights in

[5]i.e. prophets in general. See footnote 3 above.

[6]or ζητει... ἐρωτα... Or it is permissible to put the pronouns in ὑμεις ζητειτε... ὑμεις ἐρωτατε... or συ ζητει... συ ἐρωτα...

[7]or δεικνυετωσαν or φανερουτωσαν

[8]or ἀκολουθειτε

[9]or οὐκ οἰδασιν.

Section 15

Additional material.

οὐδὲ καίουσι λύχνον καὶ τιθέασι αὐτὸν ὑπὸ τὸν μόδιον ἀλλ᾽ ἐπὶ τὴν λυχνίαν, καὶ λάμπει πᾶσιν τοῖς ἐν τῇ οἰκίᾳ.   (Matthew V, 15)
Neither do they keep a lamp burning and put it under a one-peck measure but on a lamp stand, and it shines for all those in the house.
οὐδέ = neither καίω = I burn, I keep burning[10] ὁ λύχνος = an oil lamp
ὁ μόδιος = a vessel holding almost exactly a peck of grain. ἡ λυχνία = the lamp stand. λάμπω = I shine.

---

[10]"I light" (a lamp) would be ἅπτω (see Bauer, *Greek-English Lexicon of NT*, p.396).

56

Section 16

1.Being a mother, she loves her children.
2.Since it is good (*literally*, it being good), all want the wine.
3.Being bandits, you are all wicked.
4.Since he is a prophet, all listen to the blind man.
5.Since he is our friend, we tell the whole truth to the lad (*literally*, to the lad being a friend we tell the whole truth).
6.Being disciples, they follow the prophet.
7.Since the jars are clean, they fill them with water.
8.Listen to (*or*, you are listening to) the voices of the sisters[1] who are in the house.
9. He gives bread to the disciples who are in the desert (*literally*, to the being-in-the-desert disciples).

Therefore the Samaritan woman says to him "How do you, being a Jew, ask to drink from me who am a Samaritan woman (*literally*, from me being a Samaritan woman)?"

NB, the present participles of πιστεύω, τιμάω, ποιέω and δηλόω are set out in full on pp. 311-313 of An Introduction to New Testament Greek.
(a) 1.sending. (masc.) 2.knowing. (fem.) 3.seeking. (masc.) 4.examining. (masc.) 5.hating. (masc.) 6.watching. (fem.) 7.calling. (masc.) 8.diminishing. (masc.) 9.making clear. (neuter) 10.judging. (fem.) 11.feeding. (neuter). 12.finding. (fem. plu.) 13.worshipping. (masc. plu.) 14 The disciple who remains. (*literally*, the waiting disciple) 15.The teacher who walks about. 16.The one (who is) asking. 17.The man (who is) asking. 18.The maidservant who believes. 19.The maidservant who believes.[2] 20.The lad who is listening. 21.The devil which is walking about. 22.The sheep which is following. 23.The sheep which is following the shepherd.

---

[1]οὐσῶν is feminine.
[2]The difference in Greek wording does not affect the English meaning.

(b) 1.Leading. (fem)   2.The maidservant who is leading.   3.The maidservant who is leading the lambs. 4. To the believing man. 5.To the men who believe. 6.To the believing women. 7.He who follows me. (*literally* the following me (man)) 8.The shepherds who give testimony. 9.Those who give testimony. (*literally,* the testifying (men)) 10.Those who say this. 11.We know those who say these things. 12.We trust those (men) who say these things. 13.We give honour to those (women) who say these things. 14.We say nothing to those (men) who ask this.

pages 108-109

I am a voice of a man shouting in the desert: "make straight the road[3] of the Lord."

Everyone who does wicked things hates the light.

He who trusts in the son has eternal life.

For in this (respect) the word is true that one is the sower and another is the reaper.

My father gives you the true bread out of heaven. For the bread of God is (the person)[4] who descends out of heaven and gives life to the world.

The man who chews my flesh and drinks my blood remains in me and I in him.

Everyone who comes from (is out of) the truth listens to my voice.

That woman, thinking that he is the gardener, says to him, "Sir."

page 110

1. I am (being) found 2.You are baptized. (singular) 3.He/she/it is said. 4.We are held. 5.You are known. (plural) 6.They are led. 7.They are not (being) taken. 8.Surely it isn't being written, is it? 9.The disciple is (being) stoned. 10.You are sent into the temple. 11.The sheep are (being) stolen.

pages 110-111

(a)The lamb is found. 2.The bad vines are cut down.

3.The true writings are not thrown into the fire.

4.A true prophet is not understood in his fatherland.

5.We are sent into the courtyard of the temple.

---

[3]Bauer (p.554) gives this among the passages where ὁδός means "highway". Elsewhere it sometimes means "journey" and sometimes "way of life".

[4]The Greek is ambiguous because ὁ καταβαίνων could stand for ἄρτος (bread), which is a masculine noun, or for "the one who descends". Barrett (*The Gospel according to St. John* p.290) regards "the one who descends" as preferable.

6.Why are you being led into the door of the praetorium?
7.We are not judged according to the flesh.
8.We are not all offended.
9.We follow the Lord.

(b)Isn't this man the son of the carpenter? Isn't his mother called Mary and aren't his brothers Jacob (James) and Simon and Judas? And aren't all his sisters with us? Therefore where did all these things come from for this man?
Every tree which does not make good fruit (*literally*, not making good fruit) is cut down and thrown into the fire.
For the tree is known from its fruit.
page 111
Optional exercise:
1.δια τι[5] κρινεσθε; κλεπται ειναι λεγεσθε; 2.τα κακα δενδρα εἰς το του τεκτονος πυρ βαλλεται. 3.δια τον λογον εὐθυς σκανδαλιζονται. 4.πας γαρ ὁ αἰτων λαμβανει και ὁ ζητων εὑρισκει. 5.και φωνουσιν τον τυφλον λεγοντες αὐτῷ· θαρσει, ἐγειρε, φωνει σε. 6.ἠσαν ὡς προβατα μη ἐχοντα ποιμενα.

Additional material.

καὶ εἶπεν[6] Μωυσης πρὸς τὸν θεόν 'Ιδοὺ ἐγὼ ἐλεύσομαι πρὸς τοὺς υἱοὺς Ισραηλ καὶ ἐρῶ πρὸς αὐτοὺς 'Ο θεὸς τῶν πατέρων ὑμῶν ἀπέσταλκέν με πρὸς ὑμᾶς, ἐρωτήσουσίν με Τί ὄνομα αὐτῷ; τί ἐρῶ πρὸς αὐτούς; καὶ εἶπεν ὁ θεὸς πρὸς Μωυσῆν 'Εγώ εἰμι ὁ ὤν· καὶ εἶπεν Οὕτως ἐρεῖς τοῖς υἱοῖς 'Ισραηλ 'Ο ὢν ἀπέσταλκέν με. (Exodus III, 13-14) (Septuagint)
And Moses said to God, "Look, I shall go to the sons of Israel and I shall say to them 'The god of your fathers has sent me to you,' (and) they will ask me 'What is his name?' What shall I say to them?" And God said to Moses, "I am The Being One (The One Who Is);" and he said "Thus shall you say to the sons of Israel 'The Being One has sent me.' "

---

[5]or τι.
[6]For εἶπεν = he said, see section 26. ἰδού (middle imperative) = ἴδε (active imperative) ἐλεύσομαι (future middle of ἔρχομαι, section 24) = I shall come ἐρῶ (future of λέγω) = I shall say (ἐρεῖς = you will say) ἀπέσταλκεν = he has sent (perfect of ἀποστέλλω, section 29).

Section 17

page 113
1.Are you being honoured? (singular) 2.You are not loved. (plural) 3.Aren't they being filled? 4.We are being asked. 5.They are hated. 6.He/she/it is being diminished. 7.The slaves are being freed, aren't they? 8.We aren't being sought in the desert, are we? 9.How is he/she being helped? 10.Surely you aren't invited, are you? (plural) 11.The writings (the scriptures) are being examined. 12.Why is this being done? 13.Why aren't the water jars being filled? 14.Why aren't they filling the water jars?[1] 15.This[2] is not being shown to the disciples. 16.In the courtyard, we are not being watched. 17.The doorkeeper is not watching us. 18.Everything is made clear in this book. 19.The shepherds are invited to the feast.

page114
1.Are you being given? (i.e., given to some one else) (plural) 2.They are not placed. 3.They aren't being put down in the sheepfold (courtyard), are they? 4.What is being given to the shepherds? 5.What are they giving to the shepherds? 6.What is being put down here?

page 115
1.To be loosened. 2.To be received (taken). 3.To be stoned. 4.To be asked. 5.To be hated. 6.To be watched. 7.To be freed. 8.To be said (to be called (named)). 9.To bear witness. 10.To be helped.
11.These things must not be put down in the courtyard (sheepfold).

page 116
1.By the man. 2.By the mother. 3.By the wind. (*or* By (in) the spirit.) 4.By Nicodemus. 5.By the wine. 6.By the slaves. 7.By the names. 8.By the testimony.
9.The child is being baptised by you.
10.The doorkeeper is being warmed by the fire.
11.A book is being written by the woman.[3]
12.The truth is made clear by the words of the prophet.
13.Wicked men (*or* the wicked) are offended by the truth.

---

[1]active, as are no. 17, p.114, no.5, and p.115, no.9
[2]*An Introduction to New Testament Greek*, p.55, footnote 10.
[3]or possibly "by the (his) wife".

60

14.Are the blind men being invited into the house by[4] you?
15.This place is called holy by us.
page 117
1.Are you coming? (plural) 2.Are you able? (singular) 3.You are not
going. (singular) 4.They are not working. 5.The bridegroom is coming.
6.We can hear. 7.The maidservants are working. 8.The lads are coming.
9.I can testify. 10.Are you mad? (singular)
11.The head steward is going to the wedding.
12.Where can the wind blow from? 13. Can you say? (plural)
14.I cannot understand. 15.Is the farmer coming?
16.The carpenters are working.

Therefore Simon Peter comes also following him.
See, this man is baptising and all men are going to him.
Jesus comes and takes the bread and gives (it) to them and the fish likewise.
What work are you doing?[5] I am going on my way to my father.
page 119
(a)1.To work. 2.To be mad. 3.To go, proceed. 4.To fear. 5.To go to the
temple. 6.To go away from Jerusalem.[6]
7.The shepherds do not want to work in the desert.
8.The carpenters are said to be working in the house.
9.The elders do not want to go into the desert; for they consider the
prophet who lives there to be mad.
10.Who knows how to go to Capernaum?

(b)Surely he's not intending to go away to the dispersion of the Greeks and
teach the Greeks,[7] is he?

---

[4]ὑφ' represents ὑπό before a rough breathing. "You" is plural.

[5]This could, in another context, mean alternatively "why are you working?"

[6]"to come from Jerusalem" in the sense of "to originate from Jerusalem" would be ἐκ
Ἱεροσολύμων εἶναι.

[7]In Classical Greek, Ἕλλην means a person whose native language is Greek, as
compared with βάρβαρος, a person whose language and culture are not Greek. This is the
meaning at Romans I, 14, and in contemporary writers such as Josephus. In the New
Testament, Ἕλλην often means "Gentile, pagan, heathen", with reference to all persons
who came under the influence of Greek, i.e. pagan culture. In a few instances (e.g. at

Section 17

He has a devil and is mad; why are you listening to him?
His disciples were inside and Thomas (was) with them. Jesus comes ... and said, "Peace to you."

But I say to you who are listening, "Love your enemies and treat those who hate you well, pray on behalf of those who mistreat you. To the man who strikes you on the cheek offer the other one also, and from the man who takes your coat, do not keep back your under garment also. Give to everyone who asks you and do not ask for your own things back ... and if you love (delight in) those who love you, what sort of grace is it for you? For sinners also love those who love them."

Optional exercise:
1. οἱ λῃσται ὑπο του ποιμενος οὐ θεωρουνται.
2. γινωσκειν οὐ δυνασαι[8] δια τι τον κλεπτην οὐ φοβουμαι;
3. και ἀναπληρουται αὐτοις ἡ προφητεια Ἰσαιου.
4. ἐρχεται προς αὐτους περιπατων ἐπι της θαλασσης.
5. και ἐρχεται προς τους μαθητας και εὑρισκει αὐτους καθευδοντας.
6. πως ἐγειρονται οἱ νεκροι; ποιῳ δε σωματι ἐρχονται;
7. οὐ δυναται δενδρον ἀγαθον καρπους πονηρους ποιειν, οὐδε δενδρον σαπρον καρπους καλους ποιειν.
Additional material.
Προσέχετε ἀπὸ τῶν ψευδοπροφητῶν, οἵτινες ἔρχονται πρὸς ὑμᾶς ἐν ἐνδύμασιν προβάτων, ἔσωθεν δέ εἰσι λύκοι ἅρπαγες.(Matthew VII, 15)
Beware of false prophets who come to you in clothes of sheep, but inside are ravening wolves.
ὁ ψευδοπροφήτής = the false prophet ὅιτινες (literally, "whoever") here = οἵ ("who"). τὸ ἔνδυμα = the garment. ὁ λύκος = the wolf. ἅρπαξ, ἅρπαγος = ravenous (cf. ἁρπάζω I snatch, and Ἅρπυιαι, the Harpies, the "Snatchers", supernatural winged females in Greek mythology, explained in Liddell & Scott as personifications of hurricanes.)

Acts XVII, 4) it is used for "proselyte" referring to God fearing gentiles (see Bauer, p.252).
[8] or δυνασθε

pages 122-123

1.Being taken. (*or* being received) 2.Being hated. 3.Being honoured. 4.Being filled. 5.Being taken away. (*or* being raised) 6.He who is being sought. 7.She who is being known. 8.The thing which is being cut off. 9.Those (men) who are being fed. 10.Those (women) who are being found. 11.The things which are being examined. 12.Of the man who is being baptized. 13.The things which are being stolen. 14.To/for the woman who is being freed. 15.To/for the man who is being offended. 16.A man called Elias (Elijah). 17.A farmer called Nicodemus. 18.A maidservant called Mary.
19.The disciple (who is) called Peter.
20.The land called Judaea.
21.Lads called Thomas and Peter.
22.I observe the sins of the wicked being revealed.[1]
23.All the roads (that are)[2] being made straight in the desert are being made clear (revealed) to the prophet.
24.I say this to those who are called disciples of the prophet.
25.The prophet speaks to the believers (those believing); those listening to him follow him into the desert.
26.The things (which are) said by this prophet are true.

page 123

1.fearing (masc. sing. nom.) 2.proceeding (fem. sing. nom.) 3.of the man who is mad (*literally,* of the being mad (man)) 4.to/for the children who are working (*literally,* to/for the working children) 5.being able (masc. sing. nom.) to see this 6.being able (fem. plu. nom.) to do this (these things).

---

[1]= "I observe that the sins of the wicked are being revealed." In Greek, a noun clause beginning "that" which is the object of a verb equivalent in meaning to "see" or "know" is expressed by accusative and participle; e.g., "I see (I know) that you are stealing the wine" = "I see (I know) you stealing the wine" = ὁρῶ (οἶδα) σε κλέπτοντα τὸν οἶνον.

[2]αἱ ὁδοι αἱ ἐν τῇ ἐρήμῳ εὐθυνόμεναι. A different construction from no.22. NB, αἱ is the definite article "the", not the relative pronoun "which"; literally, the meaning is: "all the roads, the being made straight in the desert, are (being) revealed to the prophet." Similarly, ὁ λεγόμενος μαθητής (literally, "the (man) called a disciple" is often best expressed in English by a relative clause such as "the man who is called a disciple".

Section 18

page 124
1....so that you (singular) may see 2....so that you (plural) may not know
3.so that we may write 4....so that they may not say.
5.If we remain ... 6.If he/she does not find... 7.If you (plural) do not hear...
8.If they go away...
9.Whenever he says (she says)... 10.Whenever we do not take away (*or*
Whenever we do not raise...) 11.Whenever they steal... 12.Whenever you
(singular) do not have...
13.What are we to say? 14.What are they to write? 15.Where[3] are they to
go? 16.How are they to go away? 17.Who is to say?
18.Let us teach. 19.Let them cut off 20.Let me not see 21.May you not
hear 22.May you not find the treasure, o thieves!
23.May my words not offend.
24.May (let) the carpenter not throw the tree into the fire.
25.I put the wine in the water jar so that all may drink.
26.If we see the doorkeeper, we want to ask him where the servant girl is.
27.Whenever they cut a tree down, they throw it into the fire.
28.What are we to say? We do not know the name of this land.
page 125
This man is the heir; let us kill him.
pages 126-127
1. ...so that we may ask 2. ... so that they may not search 3. ...so that you
(plural) may know this 4. ...so that he/she may not worship 5. ...so that
he/she may not fill 6. ...so that I may set free.
7.If you (singular) give... 8.If you (plural) do not give... 9.If they do not
make clear... 10.If we place...
11.Whenever they notice... 12.Whenever we are... 13.Whenever you
(plural) hate...
14.What are we to do? 15.Who is to speak? 16.What is he/she to ask?
17.Let us see. 18.May they not observe. 19.May you (plural) not show this
to the thieves. 20.Let me give this to you. 21.Let no-one know this.
22.May your deeds be noble.
23.I am saying this to you (plural) so that you may know the truth.
24.If you notice the thief, throw him into the pool.

---

[3]Literally, "Where are they to go away to? ποῦ is used in koiné Greek for "where to"
(i.e., "whither") as well as for "where".

Section 18

25.Whenever I put bread in the courtyard, the crows come to eat it.[4]
<u>pages 127-128</u>
(a)1.We give water to those who are being sent into the desert.
2.Whenever he sees the disciples, the prophet speaks frankly (to them).
3.If you see the bandits, go away.[5]
4.If you have a bad fish, no one wants it.
5.If you have bad bread, let no one eat it.
6.What are they to do? Whenever the doorkeeper notices them, he chases them out of the house.
(b)You[6] do not want to come to me so that you may have life.
What are we to do?
If anyone walks around in the day, he does not stumble, because he sees the light of this world. But if any one walks about in the night, he does stumble, because the light is not in him.[7]
Sir, I do not have a man to put[8] me into the pool.
But they were saying this to test him, so that they might have something to accuse him of.
But this is eternal life, that they may know you, the only true God.
The man (who is) called Jesus made mud.
I came into this world so that those who do not see may see.
But Simon Peter was standing and being warmed.[9]

---

[4]The commonest way of expressing a purpose in English is to use the infinitive; this usage is also sometimes found in koiné Greek.

[5]If the ἐὰν clause expresses a contingency, ὑπάγετε is likely to be imperative. But sometimes ἐάν introduces a general condition which doesn't refer specifically to the future. Bauer (p.211) cites Luke VI, 33: ἐὰν ἀγαθοποιῆτε τοὺς ἀγαθοποιοῦντας ὑμᾶς, ποία ὑμῖν χάρις ἐστίν... ("if you do good to those who do good to you, what credit is there for you?"). Similarly, this sentence could be translated "if you see bandits, you go away".

[6]plural

[7]Barrett (*The Gospel according to St John*, p.392) notes that ancient thought did not clearly grasp the fact that vision takes place through the entry of light into the eye.

[8]For βάλλω (I throw) without a connotation of violence, see *An Introduction to New Testament Greek,* footnote 6, section 19, p.137.

[9]On p.116 of *An Introduction to New Testament Greek* it says that θερμαίνω is only found in the passive in the New Testament. On page 355 the English equivalent of θερμαίνομαι is given as "I warm myself". Liddell & Scott give only one example of the middle of θερμαίνω, from a third century B.C. papyrus: (θερμαίνεσθαι) τῇ ἐρωμένῃ

page 129
Then Pharisees and scribes from Jerusalem came to Jesus saying "Why do your disciples go against the tradition of the elders? For they do not wash their hands whenever they eat bread." But having answered he said to them, "Why do you also go against the command of God for the sake of your tradition? For God said, 'Honour your father and mother' and 'The one who speaks evil of (*or* curses) his father or mother, let him be put to death.'"

I am the true vine, and my father is the farmer. Every branch not bearing fruit he takes (it) away, and every one bearing fruit he cleanses (prunes) so that it may bear more fruit. You are already clean because of the word which I have spoken to you. Remain in me and I (will remain) in you. Just as the branch cannot bear fruit from itself unless it remains in the vine, so nor can you unless you remain in me. I am the vine, but you the branches. He who remains in me and I in him, this man bears much fruit, because without me you can do nothing.

Optional exercise:
1. μαθηται τουτου του προφητου λεγομενοι, μετ ' αὐτου ἐν τη ἐρημῳ περιπατωμεν.
2. μαθητας τουτου του προφητου λεγομενους παντες ἡμας μισουσιν.
3. μαθητων τουτου του προφητου λεγομενων, ὑφ ἡμων μηδεις σκανδαλιζηται.[10]
4. ἡμιν, μαθηταις τουτου του προφητου λεγομενοις, μηδεις κακα λεγῃ.

χαλκία δύο ὕδατος (= "to cause to be warmed two pails of water for the beloved (woman)..." When θερμαίνομαι means "I feel warmth" it is classified in Liddell & Scott as passive, e.g. Plato, Theaetetus 186B: ΣΩΚΡΑΤΗΣ. Τί οὖν δὴ ἐκείνῳ ἀποδίδως ὄνομα τῷ ὁρᾶν, ἀκούειν, ὀσφραίνεσθαι, ψύχεσθαι, θερμαίνεσθαι; ΘΕΑΙΤΗΤΟΣ. Αἰσθάνεσθαι ἔγωγε· τί γὰρ ἄλλο; (Socrates: "What name, then, do you give to seeing, hearing, smelling, feeling cold and feeling warm?" Theaetetus: "Sensation (literally, perceiving), as far as I am concerned; what else?"). Bauer does not classify θερμαίνεσθαι as middle or passive, and all the N.T. examples he cites are present or imperfect, where the middle and passive have the same form. However, he also cites Septuagint (Isaiah XLIV, 16) which is definitely passive: καὶ θερμανθεὶς εἶπεν 'Ἡδύ μοι ὅτι ἐθερμάνθην καὶ εἶδον πῦρ ("and having felt warm he said 'It was pleasant for me that I felt warm and saw a fire'").

[10]This requires σκανδαλιζηται, a verb in the present subjunctive *passive* (section 19, p. 131).

Section 18

5.ἦσαν γαρ οἱ ἐρχομενοι και οἱ ὑπαγοντες πολλοι.
6.ἐαν δὲ ἐν τῳ φωτι περιπατωμεν ὡς αὐτος ἐστιν ἐν τῳ φωτι, κοινωνιαν ἐχομεν μετ᾿ ἀλληλων.
7.παρακαλω δε ὑμας, ἀδελφοι, δια του ὀνοματος του κυριου ἡμων Ἰησου Χριστου, ἱνα το αὐτο λεγητε παντες.

Section 19

page 132
1. ...so that I may be led. 2. ...so that you (singular) may not be taken away (*or* raised). 3 ...so that he/she/it may be found. 4. ...so that we may not be sent. 5. ...so that you (plural) may be known . 6. ...so that they may not be judged. 7.If I am found ... 8.If you are sent... (singular) 9.If they are not found ... 10.If his name is not known ... 11.If the children are led into the temple ... 12.Whenever I am led into the desert... 13.Whenever you are found[1] ... (singular) 14.Whenever it is cut down ... 15.Whenever we are judged ... 16.Whenever you are sent (plural) ...17.What is to be said? 18.Let us be called noble disciples. 19.May the truth be discovered! 20.Let children be seen but not heard.

page 133
1.If I am honoured ... 2.Whenever you are helped ... (plural) 3. ... so that (he/she/)it may be shown. 4.If we are sought ... 5.Whenever they are set free ...
6.Whenever this is asked, I say nothing.
7.If you (plural) are observed by the bandits, do not run away.
8.We say this to all men so that the glory of God may not be diminished.

page 134
1. ... so that I may go on my way. 2. ... so that you may not work. (singular) 3.If he/she/it does not come ... 4.If we are afraid ... 5.Whenever they proceed ... 6. Whenever you come (go) ... (plural) 7.Let him/her not be mad ... 8.Let us all come (go). 9.Where is the shepherd to go to? For the bandits are coming.

But whenever Christ comes, no one knows where he is from.
What are we to do so that we may do the work of God?[2]

page 136
1.I judge myself. 2.Know yourself! (singular) 3.She hates herself. 4.He hates himself. 5.They glorify themselves. 6.You teach yourselves.[3]

---

[1] *or possibly,* whenever he/she/it finds... (active)

[2] "work" as a collective noun. Cf.τί ἐργάζῃ (*Introd.N.T. Greek*, section 17, p.117).

[3] Or possibly, "teach yourselves!", though often the personal pronoun is used in Greek emphatically with an imperative, e.g. ὑμεῖς ἑαυτὰς διδάσκετε! (ἑαυτὰς is feminine.)

7. They want to set themselves free.
8. He is finding his own lambs.
9. In this letter he is glorifying himself.
10. They see themselves in the water.
11. She accuses herself.
12. The carpenter is doing this work for himself.
13. The servant girl's mother is speaking on her behalf.[4]

And if I testify about myself, my testimony is true.
<u>pages 137-138</u>
Truly, truly I say to you, the man who does not come into the sheepfold of the sheep through the door, but comes up (*literally,* but coming up) from another place, is a thief and a bandit; but the one who comes in through the door is the shepherd of the sheep. To this man the doorkeeper opens (the door) and the sheep hear his voice and he calls his own sheep by name and leads them out. Whenever he leads all his own (sheep)[5] out he goes on his way in front of them and the sheep follow him, because they know his voice.

I am the good (noble) shepherd. The good shepherd lays down his life on behalf of the sheep. The hired man and one who is not a shepherd, of whom the sheep are not his own (to whom the sheep do not belong), notices the wolf coming and lets the sheep go and runs away - and the wolf seizes them and scatters them - because he is a hired man and it does not matter to him about the sheep.

I am the good shepherd and I know my own (sheep) and my own know me, just as the father knows me and I know the father, and I lay down my life on behalf of the sheep. And I have other sheep which are not out of this fold.

Because of this the father loves (delights in) me because I lay down my life, so that I may receive it again. No one takes it from me, but I lay it down of my own accord.

---

[4] αὐτῆς is not reflexive.
[5] neuter

Section 19

Optional exercise:
1.ταυτα ου ποιουμεν ίνα άγαθοι λεγωμεθα.
2.μηδενι λεγε⁶ έαν οί μαθηται έρχωνται.
3.όταν μαινηται, τα παιδαρια λεγει· δαιμονιον έχεις.
4.έαν γαρ εύαγγελιζωμαι, ούκ έστιν μοι καυχημα.
5.εί τις διακονει, ώς έξ ίσχυος ής⁷ χορηγει ό θεος, ίνα έν πασιν δοξαζηται ό θεος.
6.και όταν προσευχησθε, ούκ έσεσθε ώς οί ύποκριται, ότι φιλουσιν έν ταις συναγωγαις και έν ταις γωνιαις των πλατειων έστωτες προσευχεσθαι.

---

⁶or λεγετε.
⁷We should expect ήν, but the genitive pronoun is attracted into the genitive, the case of ίσχυος.

Section 20

page 139
1.Be known! (plural) 2.Be found! (singular) 3.Be warmed! (plural) 4.Do not be seen![1] 5.Let them not be judged according to the flesh.

Let your heart not be disturbed; you believe in God, believe also in me.[2]
page 140
1. Be noticed! (singular) 2.Be set free! (plural) 3.Let him/her/it be sought. 4.Let them be loved. 5.Let the lamb be given to the child. 6.Let the writings not be examined.
page 141
1.Work! (singular) 2.Proceed! (plural) 3.Do not come![3] 4.May he/she/it not be able to do this!

Do not be afraid, daughter of Zion.
Philip says to him, "Come and see."
Jesus says to him, "Go on your way, your son lives."
They see Jesus walking about on the sea and getting near the ship, and they were afraid. But he says to them, "It is I myself; do not be afraid."[4]
But I say to you: love (delight in, value) your enemies and pray on behalf of those who pursue you.
page 143
But a certain man was ill, Lazarus from Bethany.
And behold, there was a certain man in front of him suffering from dropsy.
A certain man was rich.
If any one loves (delights in) the world, the love of (delight in) the father is not in him.

---

[1]For the passive of βλέπω, see 2 Corinthians IV, 18: μή σκοπούντων ἡμῶν τὰ βλεπόμενα ἀλλὰ τὰ μὴ βλεπόμενα ("us not regarding the things (that are) seen but the things (that are) not seen") (cited by Bauer, p.143).
[2]For other possible translations of this sentence, see An Introduction to New Testament Greek p.94, footnote 5.
[3]i.e. "Come no more!" (see An Introduction to New Testament Greek p.225, footnote 7). It is probably unnecessary to stress the special features of the present imperative until the aorist imperative is reached.
[4]i.e. "fear no more!"

Section 20

For no one does anything in secret and seeks to be in the open himself.

Who is my mother and who are my brothers?
But as for you, who do you say that I am?[5]
And if I cast out devils in Beelzeboul,[6] as for your sons, in whom[7] do they cast (them) out?

<u>p.144</u>
(a) 1.Which man? 2.A certain man 3.Which ship? 4.A certain ship.
5.Whom do you (singular) see? 6.Whom do you (singular) hear? 7.To whom do you (singular) testify?
8.Whom are you (singular) throwing (*or* putting) into the pool?
9.We are giving the fruit to a certain blind man.
10.A certain maidservant is waiting in the temple.
11.Whose is this house?
(b)Can anything good come (be) from Nazareth?
Nathanael says to him, "From where do you know me?"
The wind blows where it wants, and you hear its sound, but you do not know where it comes from and where it is going away to.
But if I am telling you the truth, why don't you believe in me?
Go on your way, and from now onwards[8] sin no longer.
From where, then, do you have the living water?

Optional exercise:
1.ἐαν τις πονηρον τι λεγῃ, μη σκανδαλιζεσθε.[9]
2.φωνην τινος τῃ νυκτι ἀκουειν δυνασαι;[10]
3.τινα λεγουσιν οἱ ἀνθρωποι εἰναι τον υἱον του ἀνθρωπου;
4.τινος ἐχει εἰκονα και ἐπιγραφην;

---

[5] After a verb meaning "say", a noun clause beginning "that" in English can be expressed in Greek by accusative and infinitive, as here: "whom do you say me to be?"
[6] i.e., in the name of Beelzeboul.
[7] i.e., in whose name.
[8] *literally* from the now.
[9] or σκανδαλιζου.
[10] or δυνασθε.

Section 20

5.μελλει γαρ ὁ υἱος του ἀνθρωπου ἐρχεσθαι ἐν τῃ δοξῃ του πατρος αὐτου.

6.εἰ τις ἐρχεται προς με και οὐ μισει τον πατερα ἑαυτου και την μητερα και την γυναικα και τα τεκνα και τους ἀδελφους και τας ἀδελφας ἐτι τε και την ψυχην ἑαυτου, οὐ δυναται εἰναι μου μαθητης.

Additional material

(a) ὁ λύχνος τοῦ σώματος ἐστιν ὁ ὀφθαλμός σου. ὅταν ὁ ὀφθαλμός σου ἁπλοῦς ᾖ, καὶ ὅλον τὸ σῶμά σου φωτεινόν ἐστιν· ἐπὰν δὲ πονηρὸς ᾖ, καὶ τὸ σῶμά σου σκοτεινόν. σκόπει οὖν μὴ τὸ φῶς τὸ ἐν σοὶ σκότος ἐστίν. εἰ οὖν τὸ σῶμά σου ὅλον φωτεινόν, μὴ ἔχον μέρος τι σκοτεινόν, ἔσται φωτεινὸν ὅλον ὡς ὅταν ὁ λύχνος τῇ ἀστραπῇ φωτίζῃ σε.   Luke   XI,   34-36.

The lamp of the body is your eye. Whenever your eye is clear, your whole body also is full of light; but whenever it is bad, your body also (is) full of darkness. Therefore look out lest the light in you is darkness. If therefore your whole body is full of light, not having any part full of darkness, it will be full of light as when the lamp illuminates you with its brightness.
τὸ σῶμα, τοῦ σώματος = the body. ὁ ὀφθαλμός = the eye. ἁπλοῦς = single; in this context, clear, healthy. ὅλος = whole. φωτεινός = full of light. ἐπάν = as soon as (+ subjunctive). πονηρός = bad, sick. σκοτεινός = dark. σκοπέω = I look out. μή = lest[11] τὸ σκότος = darkness. τὸ μέρος = the part. ἡ ἀστραπή = bright light (originally, lightning). φωτίζω = I illuminate.

(b) καὶ εἶπεν κύριος ὁ θεὸς τῷ Νωε λέγων Ἔξελθε ἐκ τῆς κιβωτοῦ, σὺ καὶ ἡ γυνή σου καὶ οἱ υἱοί σου καὶ αἱ γυναῖκες τῶν υἱῶν σου μετὰ σοῦ καὶ πάντα τὰ θηρία, ὅσα ἐστιν μετὰ σοῦ, καὶ πᾶσα σὰρξ ἀπὸ πετεινῶν ἕως κτηνῶν, καὶ πᾶν ἑρπετὸν κινούμενον ἐπὶ τῆς γῆς ἐξάγαγε μετὰ σεαυτοῦ· καὶ αὐξάνεσθε καὶ πληθύνεσθε ἐπὶ τῆς γῆς.

Genesis VIII, 15-17 (Septuagint)
And the Lord God spoke to Noah saying, Go out of the ark (box), you and your wife and your sons and the wives of your sons with you and all the beasts, as many (as) are with you, and all flesh from birds as far as cattle,

---

[11]This is an extension of the construction μή + future indicative after a verb like "I take care that" (Bauer, p. 517, μή B, c). μή + indicative is used after σκοπεῖ to express the apprehension that something actually is the case (this passage is cited in Moulton, p.631).

and every creeping thing moving upon the earth, lead out with you; and
increase and be multiplied upon the earth.

εἶπεν = said (see section 26) ἔξελθε = go out! (strong aorist imperative,
see section 26). ἡ κιβωτός = box, chest, coffer (used in Septuagint both for
Noah's and Moses' ark). τὸ θηρίον = the (wild) animal, the beast. τὸ
πετεινόν = the bird ("the flying thing", from πέτομαι = I fly). τὸ κτῆνον
= the domesticated animal. τὸ ἐρπετόν = the creeping animal (ἕρπω = I
creep). ἕως (here) = as far as. κινέομαι = I move. ἐξάγαγε = lead out!
(strong aorist imperative of ἐξάγω, for which see section 26). αὐξάνομαι
(passive) = I increase (literally, I am increased). πληθύνω = I multiply.

Section 21

1.We were seeing (*or* We used to see)[1]. 2.You were writing (plural) (*or* You used to write). 3.You were teaching yourself (*or* You used to teach yourself). 4.I was judging (*or* I used to judge). 5.He/she/it was taking (*or* He/she/it used to take). 6.The disciples were staying. 7.You were believing. (singular) 8.The shepherd was fleeing. 9.The carpenter was sending the lad to the temple. 10.Did you understand? (most probably in the sense of "used you to understand?")[2] (plural). 11.We were throwing.

1.You were shouting. (plural) 2.Were we showing? 3.I was calling. 4.You were hating. (plural) 5.You hate. (plural)[3] 6.You were blowing. (singular) 7.We were testifying. 8.The wind was blowing. 9.Used you (plural) to hate us? 10.The prophet was speaking. 11.Was the maidservant calling?

12.The doorkeeper was searching for (seeking) the thief.

13.The shepherds were watching the sheep.

14.The farmers were showing us the way.

1.We were leading 2.You were taking. (singular) 3.We were loving (delighting in). 4.You were asking a question. (plural) 5.I help.[4] 6.I was helping. 7.You were making smaller. (singular)

8.The Jews were examining the scriptures.

9.The disciples were following.

10.Were the lads listening to the farmer shouting?

---

[1]See *An Introduction to New Testament Greek*, page 147. In most of the exercises, the past continuous form ("I was ... ") and the past continual form ("I used to ... ") are equally appropriate, and after the first few examples, only one will be given in the manual.

[2]For the difference between the imperfect and aorist tenses, see p.193. "I understood" would usually be imperfect; "I came to understand", i.e., "it (suddenly) dawned on me" would be aorist.

[3]present

[4]present

11.The mother could not find her child.[5]
12.The farmers were making the road straight.

pages152-3

Imperfect of verbs prefixed with a preposition:

1.We were walking about. 2.You were worshipping. (singular) 3.I was accusing *or* They were accusing. 4.Are they accusing?[6] 5.You are walking about.[7] (singular) 6.He/she/it was walking about. 7.We were making smaller. 8.We were cutting the trees down. 9.Were you (plural) opening the door?

10.The doorkeepers were opening the door.

11.John had one brother.

12.The hired men could see the thief coming; therefore they were not intending to stay.

pages153-4

He was staying there with them and baptizing.

Jesus himself was not baptizing, but his disciples (were).

And for this reason the Jews were pursuing (i.e., persecuting) Jesus, because he used to do these things on the Sabbath. But Jesus answered them, "My father is working until now, and I am working." For this reason the Jews were seeking to kill him all the more, because he was not only breaking the Sabbath, but also used to call God his own father, making himself equal to God.

But he was meaning Judas Iscariot[8] (the son of) Simon; for this man, who was one of the twelve, was intending[9] to betray him.

---

[5]literally, "was not finding her child" For lack of augment, see *An Introduction to New Testament Greek* p.151, footnote 1.

[6]present

[7]present

[8]So Textus Receptus: ἔλεγε δὲ τὸν Ἰούδαν Σίμωνος Ἰσκαριώτην. But Nestle-Aland has ἔλεγεν δὲ τὸν Ἰούδαν Σίμωνος Ἰσκαριώτου ("but he was mentioning Judas the son of Simon Iscariot"). Metzger, *A Textual Commentary on the Greek New Testament*, p. 215, says that the genitive case, Ἰσκαριώτου, agreeing with Σίμωνος, is to be preferred to the accusative case Ἰσκαριώτην agreeing with Ἰούδαν "on the basis of preponderant external evidence".

[9]μέλλω is rarely found in koiné Greek with the future infinitive, though that is usual in Classical (Attic) Greek. When it is, it is very emphatic, meaning "will certainly..." It is often found in koiné with the present infinitive (as here), when it either means "I intend

And after this, Jesus used to go about[10] in Galilee; for he did not wish to go about in Judaea, because the Jews were seeking to kill him.

pages155-6

1.The large kingdom. 2.The great prophet. 3.The large temple. 4.Much frankness. 5.Much wine. 6.Of the large pool. 7.Many mothers. 8.Of many bridegrooms. 9.For many nights.[11] 10.With a loud voice. 12.I see many thieves.

page156

In the house of my father there are many apartments.[12]

I still have many things to say to you, but you are unable to bear (them) now.

And while[13] he was in Jerusalem at the Passover festival, many came to believe in his name, seeing his signs[14] which he was doing.

page157 It should be pointed out here that after a verb such as say, know, think or their equivalents, introducing an indirect statement,[15] in Greek the clause beginning ὅτι normally has a verb in the same tense as the direct speech. For instance, *he was saying that the prophet was walking about in the courtyard* becomes ἔλεγεν ὅτι ὁ προφήτης περιπατεῖ ἐν τῇ αὐλῇ, since what he said was "the prophet is walking about in the courtyard". Therefore ὁ δὲ εἶπεν ὅτι προφήτης ἐστι can be translated either as *indirect speech*

                - he said that he was a prophet -

or as *direct speech*

                - he said "He is a prophet" -

as has been done on p.157 0f *An Introduction to New Testament Greek*. There are, however, clear examples in the gospels where ὅτι is used to

---

to" or "I am destined to", or is simply a periphrasis for the future and means only "I am going to". (Bauer, pp 500-1)

[10]literally, "walk about".

[11]expression of time; see *An Introduction to New Testament Greek*, section 13, p.84.

[12]"rooms" - RSV.

[13]For ὡς, see *An Introduction to New Testament Greek*, section 25, p.194 (vocabulary). It can mean "while" as well as "as".

[14]See page 39 (above), footnote 5.

[15]i.e., a noun clause beginning "that" in English.

introduce *direct* speech; e.g. John X 36: ὑμεῖς λέγετε ὅτι βλασφημεῖς, where the English equivalent is *You say "You are blaspheming."* (See also the example from John IX 9, below.) In such cases, ὅτι must be omitted when translating into English and quotation marks must be used (see Bauer, p.589).

page158

Many therefore out of the crowd, having heard the word, began to say "This is truly the prophet."

Therefore they began to say to him, "Who are you?"

Therefore the Jews were seeking him at the festival, and were saying, "Where is that man?" And there was much secret discussion[16] about him in the crowds. Some were saying, "He is a good man." Others were saying, "No, but[17] he leads the people astray." However, no one spoke openly because of the fear of the Jews.

So the neighbours and those who noticed before that he was blind,[18] said, "Isn't this the man who used to sit and beg?" Some said, "This is (the man). But others said, "He is like him." That man said, "I am he."

Optional exercise:

1. ὁ πατηρ μου ἐν τῳ οἰκῳ ἐμενε ὁτι ἠσθενει.

2. τους προφητας ἐτιμωμεν και ἐν τῳ ἰερῳ προσεκυνουμεν.

3. μεγα ἐργον ἠν παντα τα προβατα εὑρισκειν. πολλα αὑτων ἐν τῃ ἐρημῳ περιεπατει.

4. ἠγγιζεν δε ἡ ἑορτη των ἀζυμων ἡ λεγομενη πασχα.

5. ἠκουον δε ταυτα παντα οἱ Φαρισαιοι φιλαργυροι ὑπαρχοντες και ἐξεμυκτηριζον αὑτον.

6. και παντες ἐμαρτυρουν αὑτῳ και ἐθαυμαζον ἐπι τοις λογοις της χαριτος τοις ἐκπορευομενοις ἐκ του στοματος αὑτου και ἐλεγον· οὑχι υἱος ἐστιν Ἰωσηφ οὑτος;

---

[16] See *An Introduction to New Testament Greek*, p. 157, footnote 21.

[17] ἀλλά can also mean "rather", introducing the main point after an objection (see Bauer, p.38)

[18] Textus Receptus has τυφλὸς ("blind"); Nestle-Aland has προσαίτης ("a beggar"). There are various ways of translating this verse. Zerwick and Grosvenor translate ὅτι ...ἠν as "when he was a beggar", but Barrett (p.359) refers to John IV, 35 "behold the fields that they are white for harvest", a parallel example where the subject of a ὅτι clause has been moved to the clause governing it, to become an object. (e.g., "I know thee who thou art.")

Section 22

page 161
1.I was being said.[1] 2.You were being thrown. (singular) 3.It was being written. 4.We were being understood. 5.They were being judged.
6.The farmer was being sent. 7.The lads were being sent. 8.The slaves were being released. 9.The fruit was being harvested. 10.Were you warming yourself, doorkeeper?[2]
11.The lambs were being taken by the bandit.
12.Were you being troubled, disciples?
page162
1.I was being taken away. 2.You were being found. (singular) 3.It was being made straight. 4.We were being led. 5.You were being awakened. (plural)
6.Where were you (plural) being led away to by the thieves?
7.The sons of Zebedee were called James and John.

Verbs prefixed with a preposition:
1.The servant girl was called Mary.
2.The trees were being cut down by the farmers.
3.The doors of the temple were being opened.
4.What were you (plural) called in your fatherland?
page164
1.I was being hated. 2.You were being set free. (singular) 3.He/she was being asked. 4.We were being called. 5.You were being requested.[3] (plural)
6.They were being worshipped.
7.Nathanael's mother was being helped by her daughter.[4]
8.The servant girls were not being invited to the wedding.

---

[1] *or,* I was being called, I used to be called (see *An Introduction to New Testament Greek*, section 16, p.110)

[2] *literally,* "were you being warmed?" (see p.65 above, footnote 9)

[3] *or* (middle) you asked for yourselves.

[4] ἡ θυγάτηρ is given as a new word on p.165 of *An Introduction to N.T. Greek*.

9.Wicked men, you were (being) revealed by your deeds! Now you are hated[5] by every one.

(imperfect passive of δίδωμι and τίθημι)
1.Were we being put? 2.It was being put, wasn't it? 3.They weren't being put, were they?
4.We were being betrayed to the Romans by our enemies.
5.The life of the good (noble) shepherd was being laid down on behalf of the sheep.

page165
NB(1) The same rules for augments apply to deponent as to other verbs; so the initial ε of ἔρχομαι is lengthened to η in the imperfect tense.
NB(2) The use of the prefix ε to indicate that the tense of a verb is past has the grammatical name "syllabic augment". The use of a long vowel as a prefix to indicate a past tense is called "temporal augment". In general, verbs whose stems begin with a consonant have the syllabic augment (ε) and verbs whose stems begin with vowels have the temporal augment (a long vowel). However, in a few cases, verbs whose stems begin with a consonant are sometimes found with the *temporal* augment instead of the *syllabic* augment.   So both ἐδύναμην and ἠδύναμην are found for "I was able". The other example cited by Moulton (*A Treatise on the Grammar of New Testament Greek* , p. 82) is ἤμελλον ("I was about (to)") which is found as an alternative to ἔμελλον. Moulton notes that both of these are old Attic usages, i.e. coming down from the Classical Greek in use in 5th century BC Athens.

1.I was[6] mad. 2.Were you afraid? (singular) 3.We were working.
4.Were you (plural) going on your way? 5.Weren't you (plural) able to do this? 6.Aren't they coming?[7]
7.He was becoming blind. 8.Why was the child afraid?
9.On the first day the daughter of the prophet was coming..
10.How many carpenters were working in the temple?

---

[5]present
[6]The imperfect represents a condition that went on for some time.
[7]present

11.We were going on our way before (i.e. in front of) the bridegroom.
page166
They were both arriving and being baptized.
Therefore the Jews were fighting against[8] each other saying, "How is he able to give us his flesh to eat?"
But[9] there is in Jerusalem near the sheep gate a pool which is called in Hebrew "Bethzatha", which has five porches.
And Jesus was walking around in the temple, in the porch of Solomon.
But there was a man there and his right hand was withered. And the scribes and Pharisees were watching him carefully (to see) if he would heal (him) on the Sabbath.
Blind men receive their sight, lame men walk around,
lepers are purified, and deaf men hear,
dead men are raised, poor people are preached to.
page169
(a)1.While the teacher was writing letters, the lads were talking to each other.
2.When the prophet was staying in the desert, we saw the disciples healing the palsied man.
3.While the slaves were working in the courtyard, the woman was looking for the drachma.
4.While the woman was searching the house, the child was showing her the drachma.
5.The head steward was troubled because the wine was running short.

(b)Because a strong wind was blowing, the sea was getting rough.
But he was saying this indicating by what sort of death he was going to die.
But Jesus was going on his way with them. And when he (Jesus) was now (already) not far from the house, the centurion sent friends saying to him, "Master, do not trouble yourself."[10]

---

[8]This is an additional meaning of πρός to those given in section 8. Bauer notes (p.710) that πρός can be used to denote relationships, e.g. "with hostility to" (as here) or "friendly to".
[9]The meaning of this "but" is not clear. Barrett, *The Gospel according to St. John* p.249, notes that the text of this verse is somewhat disordered.
[10]The passive of σκύλλω means "I trouble myself".

Section 22

If you were blind, you would not have sin; but now you say "We see", (and) your sin remains.
If this man were not from beside God, he would be able to do nothing.[11]
If God were your father, you would love me.

Optional exercise:
1.σου ταυτα λεγοντος[12] οὐκ ἐσκανδαλιζομεθα.
2.εἰ το δενδρον καρπον ἀγαθον εἰχεν, οὐκ ἀν ἐξεκοπτετο και εἰς το πυρ ἐβαλλετο.
3.εἰ οἱ ποιμενες τους ἀμνους μη ἐζητουν, ἐν τῃ ἐρημῳ οὐκ ἀν περιεπατουν.
4.και ἐξεπλησσοντο ἐπι τῃ διδαχῃ αὐτου· ἠν γαρ διδασκων αὐτους ὡς ἐξουσιαν ἐχων και οὐκ ὡς οἱ γραμματεις.
5.και ἐπορευοντο οἱ γονεις αὐτου κατ ' ἐτος εἰς 'Ιερουσαλημ τῃ ἐορτῃ του πασχα.
6.και ἐρχονται παλιν εἰς 'Ιεροσολυμα.[13] και ἐν τῳ ἱερῳ περιπατουντος αὐτου ἐρχονται προς αὐτον οἱ ἀρχιερεις και οἱ γραμματεις και οἱ πρεσβυτεροι και ἐλεγον αὐτῳ· ἐν ποια ἐξουσια ταυτα ποιεις;

---

[11]For double negatives, see *An Introduction to New Testament Greek*, section 13, p.85.
[12]or ὑμων ταυτα λεγοντων
[13]There is no uniformity about the Greek for Jerusalem.

Section 23

pages171-2
1.You will believe. (plural) 2.They will not believe. 3.Shall we believe?
4.He/she/it will bring. 5.They will see. 6.You will write. (singular)
7.You are writing.[1] (singular) 8.Shall I send? 9.He/she/it will send.
10.The farmer will believe. 11.We shall believe in the prophet. 12.He is
going away[2] into the desert. 13.We shall send the lad. 14.We shall bring
the sheep. 15.You will have[3] one drachma. (singular) 16.They will pursue
the wolves.

pages172-3
1.You will seek. (singular) 2.I shall honour. 3.He/she/it will show. 4.We
shall worship. 5.We ask.[4] 6.Will you call? (plural) 7.You will help.
(singular) 8.He/she will love (delight in).
9.The farmer will shout. 10.Will the worshippers fill the temple?
11.The centurion will show us the praetorium.
12.Will you (singular) make this smaller? 13.Shall we see the festival?
14.The teacher is not calling the lads. I shall call them.
15.Where will Christ come from? Nobody knows.

And on that day you will not ask me anything.
Go away into Judaea so that your disciples also shall see the deeds which
you are doing.
What shall I do, because I do not have (a place) where I shall collect my
crops.[5]

page174 *(top)*[6]
1.We shall judge. 2.We judge. 3.They will judge. 4.Will they judge? 5.I
shall take away. 6.You will take away. (singular) 7.He/she will kill. 8.We
shall kill. 9.He/she is killing. 10.Will you kill? (singular) 11.Will you

---

[1]present
[2]present
[3]NB rough breathing in the future tense; see *An Introduction to New Testament Greek*,
footnote on p.171.
[4]present
[5]literally, fruits.
[6]This exercise is a comparison between present and future forms.

(plural) wake him? 12.Are you (plural) waking him? 13.We are announcing this. 14.They will announce this. 15.We shall not take away. 16.Won't you take away? (plural)

page174 (bottom)

1.They will be ill. 2.We shall do. 3.You will find. (singular) 4.He/she will give. 5.Will he/she speak? 6.We shall announce. 7.You will love (delight in). (plural) 8.They will seek. 9.Will you ask? (plural) 10.He/she will put. 11.I shall not worship. 12.He/she will not kill. 13.You (singular) will have bread. 14.You have[7] a demon. (singular) 15.Nothing will bother me.

page175

1.The large mountains. 2.In the mountains. 3.Of the nation. 4.By (or to or for) the nation. 5.All the nations. 6.In the crowd. 7.With the crowd.
8.The prophet is going away to the mountains.
9.We must[8] worship on this mountain.
10.A crowd of worshippers was in the temple.

pages176-7

Everything which the father is giving to me will come to me.

You[9] will search for me and you will not find me, and where I am (or possibly where I shall go) you cannot come.

So the Jews said to themselves, "Where is this man intending to go that we shall not find him? Surely he doesn't intend to go to the Dispersion of (i.e. among) the Greeks[10] and teach the Greeks? What is this word which he said, 'You will search for me and you will not find me, and where I am you cannot come'?"

So the Jews began to say, "Surely he won't kill himself, will he, because he says, 'Where I am going to, you cannot come'?"

The man (person) who chews my flesh and drinks my blood has eternal life, and I shall raise him up on the last day.

---

[7]present

[8]it binds us to, it is necessary for us to...

[9]plural; also at John VII, 35-36 and VIII, 22.

[10] Barrett, *The Gospel according to St. John*, p.325, citing Bultmann, *The Gospel of John*, p.309 (tr. Beasley-Murray, Hoare & Riches, Westminster Press, Philadelphia, 1971) takes the genitive τῶν ʽΕλλήνων as "a genitive of direction" referring to the place where the dispersed people are found, rather than as a genitive referring to the dispersed people themselves. Bauer (p.252) takes ʽΕλληνες here to mean "Gentiles, pagan, heathen", not (as at John XII, 20 and Acts XVII, 4) Greek speaking proselytes.

But if you do not believe in the writings of that man[11] how will you believe in my words?

Jesus answered and said to her, "Everyone who drinks from this water will be thirsty again; but the man who may drink from the water which I shall give to him will never be thirsty to eternity, but the water which I shall give to him will become in him a well of water leaping up into eternal life." The woman says to him, "Sir, give me this water, so that I may not thirst and come here by a roundabout way to draw water." He says to her, "Go away, call your husband and come here." The woman answered and said to him, "I do not have a husband."

Optional exercise:

1.οὐδεις ὑδωρ ἀπο ταυτης της πηγης ἀντλησει.

2.την ἀληθειαν ἐν ταις γραφαις εὑρησομεν;

3.ἐαν ὁ γεωργος ἐρχηται, τι ποιησει;

4.λεγει αὐτῳ· ἐκ του στοματος σου κρινω σε, πονηρε δουλε.

5.τινα δε ἐξ ὑμων τον πατερα αἰτησει ὁ υἱος ἰχθυν, και ἀντι ἰχθυος ὀφιν αὐτῳ ἐπιδωσει;

6.οὐ φονευσεις, οὐ μοιχευσεις, οὐ κλεψεις, οὐ ψευδομαρτυρησεις. τιμα τον πατερα και την μητερα, και ἀγαπησεις τον πλησιον σου ὡς σεαυτον.

---

[11]i.e., Moses

Section 24

page180 (top)
1.Shall we see? 2.You will not see. (plural) 3.You see.[1] (singular) 4.You will see. (singular) 5.Won't he/she see?
6.The disciples will see the truth.
7.The hired man will see the wolf coming.
page 180 (centre)
1.He/she will know. They will live. You will take. (singular) Shall I hear?
2.You will not understand. (singular) 3.The bandits will not live.
4.Won't you (plural) take the drachmas? 5.The farmer will see you.[2]
page181
1.Will you die? (singular) 2.Will he/she die? 3.You will not die. (plural)
4.You are not dying.[3] (plural) 5.We shall not all die. 6.You will die in your sins. (plural)
7.Will the prophet die?

And now, therefore, you have grief; but I shall see you again, and your heart will be made glad, and no one is taking[4] your joy[5] away from you. And on that day you will not ask me anything. Truly, truly I am saying to you if you ask[6] the father for anything in my name he will give it to you.

---

[1]present
[2]singular
[3]present
[4]the present tense is sometimes used in anticipation in Greek, as in English.
[5]ἡ χαρά = joy (see word list, p.366, and section 28, p.239).
[6]Instead of ἐάν τι αἰτήσετε (future indicative), read, with Nestle-Aland, ἄν (= ἐάν) τι αἰτήσητε (aorist subjunctive) (for which see *An Introduction to New Testament Greek*, section 25, p.199) (= if you request anything ...). Textus Receptus has ὅσα ἄν αἰτήσητε (= however many things you may request ...). (It is not certain whether ἐάν τι αἰτήσετε is correct koiné Greek or not. Moulton (p.369) noted that ἐάν is sometimes joined with the indicative, and gives as an example John VIII, 36 ἐὰν ὁ υἱὸς ὑμᾶς ἐλευθερώσει (= if the son shall set you free), but now the Nestle-Aland text has ἐλευθερώσῃ (aorist subjunctive), which is the normal construction. Of Moulton's examples of ἐάν with the future indicative, however, at least one still seems possibly right. At Luke XI, 12, where Nestle-Aland has ἢ καὶ αἰτήσει ᾠόν (= or he will also request an egg ...), the apparatus criticus shows that several ancient mss. including the

Section 24

page182
(a)1.You will proceed. (singular) 2.He/she/it will come. 3.We shall become (*or* happen). 4.We are becoming (*or* happening).[7] 5.Do we know? 6.We shall know. 7.Will you become (*or* happen)? (singular) 8.You will know. (singular) 9.Will he/she/it be? 10.They will not be 11.You will not be. (singular) 12.Where will the true prophets come from? 13.How shall I know the truth? 14.Where will the great festival happen?

(b)1.They will see. 2.He/she/it will become (*or* happen). 3.Will you hear? (singular) 4.They will know. 5.You (plural) will take. 6.They will die. 7.You will come. (singular) 8.Come![8] (singular) 9.Will he/she/it die? 10.We shall not proceed. 11.Shall we not hear? 12.He/she/it will not become (*or* happen). 13.He/she/it will not know. 14.These sheep will not hear your voice. 15.Surely all the lame people will not come within one day, will they? 16.If you follow the prophet, you will be true disciples.

page183
The man who chews this bread will live to eternity.
I am going away and you will search for me, and you will die in your sinfulness.
If you remain in my word, truly you are my disciples; and you will know the truth and the truth will make you free.
Where I am, there will my servant be also.

page185
1.Will you be loved (delighted in)?[9] (plural) 2.Truly we shall be saved. 3.Will you be (made) glad, disciple? 4.The water pot will be shattered.

Chester Beatty papyrus and Codex Alexandrinus have ἐὰν καὶ ᾠὸν αἰτήσει (= if he will also request an egg).)
[7]present (as also no.5).
[8]present imperative
[9]ἀγαπηθήσεσθε. ἀγαπήσεσθε (middle) was a misprint in the first printing of *An Introduction to New Testament Greek*. It would mean "you will delight in for yourselves" but is not attested.

5.The mothers of the lads will be grieved.

6.Will those who say these things be loved?

7.Whenever the wolves come, how will the sheep be saved by the good shepherd?

<u>pages 185-7</u>

Truly, truly I say to you that an hour is coming and now is when the corpses will hear the voice of the son of God and ... will live.

Do not be amazed[10] at this, that an hour is coming in which all those (who are) in the tombs will hear his voice and will make their way out.

I have come in the name of my father, and you do not receive me; if someone else (another man) comes in his own name, you will receive him (that man).

And they will all be taught by[11] God.

And I shall ask the father, and he will give you another helper to remain with you for ever, the spirit of truth, whom the world cannot accept, because it does not see him (n)or know him; you know him, because he stays beside you and will be in you.

The woman says to him, "Sir, I observe that you are a prophet. Our fathers worshipped on this mountain and you say that in Jerusalem is the place where it is necessary to worship. Jesus says to her, "Believe me, lady, that an hour is coming when neither on this mountain nor in Jerusalem will you worship the father.[12] You worship what you do not know; we worship what we know, because salvation is from the Jews. But an hour is coming and now is, when the true worshippers will worship the father in spirit and in truth; for indeed[13] the father seeks such people who worship him.[14] God is a spirit; and those who worship him must worship (him) in spirit

---

[10]Really, "henceforth do not be amazed..." See *An Introduction to New Testament Greek*, section 27, p.225, footnote 7.

[11]One could say that ὑπό is understood, although perhaps it is better to say that the function of a preposition is really only to help to see the exact meaning of a case; moreover, this passage is possibly meant to be in an antique style since it is a quotation from or a reference to Septuagint. See also the fuller note on p. 115 below.

[12]προσκυνέω is found with both the accusative and the dative.

[13]καὶ γάρ, used to introduce an explanation. (See Bauer, and Zerwick & Grosvenor.)

[14]"wants people of this kind as his worshippers" (Zerwick & Grosvenor). The translation is difficult, and students may get to it by "seeks such the worshipping-him people" i.e. "people like this who worship him".

and in truth." The woman says to him, "I know that Messiah is coming (the one called Christ); when that one comes, he will announce everything to us." Jesus says to her, "I am (he), the one speaking to you."

The poor in spirit are fortunate because the kingdom of the heavens[15] is theirs.
Those who grieve are fortunate, because they will be strengthened.
The humble are fortunate because they will acquire the earth.[16]
Those who hunger and thirst for righteousness are fortunate because they will be satisfied.
The merciful are fortunate because they themselves will receive mercy.
The pure in heart are fortunate, because they themselves will see God.
The peacemakers are fortunate, because they themselves will be called sons of God.

Optional exercise:
1.λεγω δε ὑμιν ὁτι πολλοι ἀπο ἀνατολων και δυσμων ἡξουσιν και ἀνακλιθησονται μετα ʼΑβρααμ και ʼΙσαακ και ʼΙακωβ ἐν τη βασιλεια των οὐρανων, οἱ δε υἱοι της βασιλειας ἐκβληθησονται εἰς το σκοτος το ἐξωτερον.
2.οὐδεις δυναται δυσι κυριοις δουλευειν· ἡ γαρ τον ἑνα μισησει και τον ἑτερον ἀγαπησει, ἡ ἑνος ἀνθεξεται και του ἑτερου καταφρονησει.

---

[15]See Bauer, p.594. "The plural is usually used in Greek to indicate the abode of the divine"; however, Bauer also notes that οὐρανός is always singular in St. John's Gospel.
[16]As opposed to heaven; cf Genesis I, 1 (Septuagint): ἐν ἀρχῇ ἐποίησεν ὁ θεὸς τὸν οὐρανὸν καὶ τὴν γῆν. Further, at Genesis I, 10,, when the waters under the heavens had been collected into their reservoirs and dry land appeared, Septuagint says: καὶ ἐκάλεσεν ὁ θεὸς τὴν ξηρὰν γῆν.

Section 25

1.I saw. 2.I wrote. 3.I sent. 4.You wrote. (singular) 5.Did he believe?
6.We sent. 7.You saw. (plural) 8.We troubled. 9.You did not sit down.
(singular) 10.They wrote. 11.I was writing *or* they were writing.[1] 12.The
slave saw *or* the slave looked. 13.You (singular) wrote the book. 14.Did
you (plural) see the sign? 15.He sent his son to the temple. 16.They did not
trust each other.[2] 17.They did not come to trust each other.

-αω, -εω and -οω verbs

1.I honoured. 2.I did *or* I made. 3.I showed. 4.I sought. 5.You testified.
(singular) 6.He/she/it came to hate. 7.We shouted. 8.You filled. (plural)
9.They noticed. 10.Did he/she speak? 11.Did I make clear?
12.The prophet spoke. 13.He made the truth clear. 14.We were looking
for[3] the drachma. 15.Did I lead the crowd astray?

verbs with prepositions prefixed:

1.προσκυνέω   2.διατρίβω   3.περιπατέω   4.ἐκκόπτω   5.κατηγορέω
6.ἀνοίγω.
1.We worshipped. 2.You remained. (singular) 3.He/she walked about.
4.You accused. (plural) 5.They cut down. (past)
6.He/she worshipped the true God.
7.Did they walk about in the courtyard?
8.The prophet himself opened the door of the courtyard and invited the lad
into the feast.

1.ἀκούω   2.ἐρωτάω   3.ὠφελέω   4.ἐλευθερόω   5.ἀκολουθέω.

1.He/she helped. 2.We asked. 3.You loved. (plural) 4.They freed. 5.Did I
hear? 6.The Jews searched the scriptures. 7.Did the sheep follow the
shepherd?

---

[1]imperfect
[2]imperfect
[3]imperfect

Section 25

page 193
1.He/she sent out. 2.You took away. (singular) 3.They indicated. 4.We waited. 5.You judged. (plural) 6.I aroused.[4]
7.Did you (plural) take the water pot away?
8.The prophet sent the whole nation out into the desert.

Aorists and imperfects:
1.I was waiting *or* They were waiting. (imperfect) 2.I waited. (aorist) 3.He/she was honouring. (imperfect) 4.He/she honoured. (aorist) 5.I was feeling ill *or* They were feeling ill. (imperfect) 6.They fell ill. (aorist) 7.You heard. (aorist) (plural) 8.You were hearing/you used to hear. (imperfect) (plural) 9.I killed. (aorist) 10.I was killing *or* They were killing. (imperfect) 11.You were thirsty. (imperfect) (plural) 12.You became thirsty. (aorist) (plural) 13.We testified. (aorist) 14.We were testifying. (imperfect) 15.I was cutting down *or* They were cutting down. (imperfect) 16.They cut down. (aorist)

page 194
Jesus made this beginning of the miracles (signs) in Cana in[5] Galilee and revealed his glory, and his disciples came to believe in him.
But as he was in Jerusalem in the Passover in the feast,[6] many people came to believe in his name because they saw the miracles (signs) which he was doing.
They bring him to the Pharisees, the man who was formerly blind. And it was Sabbath on the day when Jesus made the mud and opened his eyes. So again the Pharisees also kept on asking him how he received his sight.[7]

---

[4]The Greek should be διήγειρα. διέγειρα was a misprint in the first printing.

[5]*literally* "of", but the genitive is sometimes used to express relations of place, e.g. εἰς τὰς κώμας Καισαρείας τῆς Φιλίππου (= into the villages around Caesarea Philippi) (Mark VIII, 27) (cited by Moulton, p.234).

[6]i.e., at the Passover feast.

[7]We should probably prefer to say "had made", "had opened" and "had received", but Greek tends to avoid the pluperfect (the "had" tense in English) and prefers the aorist. (See *An Introduction to New Testament Greek*, section 30, p.267.)

After this Jesus showed himself again to the disciples near the sea of Tiberias.

He pulled the net to land full of large fish, a hundred and fifty three (of them).

page 195

NB The example given in *An Introduction to New Testament Greek* (οἱ ἀκούσαντες or αἱ ἀκούσασαι= those who had heard) is only correct in a past context, e.g., οἱ ἀκούσαντες τοῦτον τὸν λόγον ἐθαύμασαν (= those who *had* heard this story were amazed). If the context is present or future, οἱ ἀκούσαντες or αἱ ἀκούσασαι = those who *have* heard. cf. *An Introduction to New Testament Greek* p.198: καὶ ἐπορεύσονται οἱ τὰ ἀγαθὰ ποιήσαντες εἰς ἀνάστασιν ζωῆς (= and those who have done good things will come forth to a resurrection of life).

page 196

1.Having observed the sign, all came to believe.

2.Having opened the door, the maidservant called the doorkeeper.

3.We saw the wolf after it had killed the lamb.[8]

4.The woman will give a drachma to the lad who did this.[9]

5.The father of the lad who helped the woman is a farmer.[10]

6.I know none of those who stole the sheep.[11]

7.The prophet said this to those who had followed him into the desert.[12]

But there was, being ill, a certain man,[13] Lazarus from Bethany, from the village of Mary and Martha her sister. And it was Mary who had anointed[14] the Lord with ointment and wiped his feet with her hair, whose brother Lazarus was ill. So the sisters sent away to him saying, "Lord, see,

---

[8]literally, We saw the having-killed-the-lamb wolf.

[9]literally, The woman will give a drachma to the having-done-this boy.

[10]literally, The father of the having-helped-the-woman lad is a farmer.

[11]literally, I know none of the having-stolen-the-sheep (men).

[12]literally, The prophet said these things to the having-followed-him-into-the-desert (men).

[13]or better, There was a certain man who was ill ...,

[14]literally, And it was Mary, the having-anointed-the-Lord with myrrh and having-wiped-his-feet with her hair (woman) ...

(he) whom you love is ill." But when he had heard this,[15] Jesus said, "This illness is not to do with death but for the sake of the glory of God."
For Jesus himself bore witness that a prophet does not have honour in his native land.
page198 *(For the declension of ἡ πόλις see Introd. to NT Greek, p. 342)*
1.Hail, O king! 2.The maidservant was following the king.
3.The king is speaking to the priests.
4.Who accepts the teaching of this scribe (scholar)?
5.All men fear the high priest.
6.The lame man was waiting for the movement of the water.
7.Why didn't you (singular) stay in the city?
8.Surely the parents of the blind man didn't want to answer the priest when he was asking this, did they?

An hour is coming in which all who are in the tombs will hear his voice and will make their way out - those who have done good things to a resurrection of life[16] but those who have done evil things to a resurrection of judgement.
Therefore Simon Peter who had a sword drew it and struck the slave of the high priest and cut off the outer part of his right ear. And the name of the slave was Malchus.
page 199
NB A simple rule would be that the present subjunctive is used for actions which are continuing or repeated, and the aorist for those which are simple and isolated. E.g., John III, 17: οὐ γὰρ ἀπέστειλεν ὁ θεὸς τὸν υἱὸν εἰς τὸν κόσμον ἵνα κρίνῃ (present active subjunctive) τὸν κόσμον ἀλλ' ἵνα σωθῇ (aorist passive subjunctive) ὁ κόσμος δι' αὐτοῦ (= "God did not send his son into the world so that he might (ever) condemn the world but so that the world might be saved once-for-all (aorist passive subjunctive) through the agency of him"). (In practice, the aorist subjunctive was clearly the usual one, and not all examples of aorist subjunctives are so clear cut: e.g. John IV, 34 seems to use aorist subjunctives to make a general statement - ἐμὸν βρῶμα ἐστιν ἵνα ποιήσω

---

[15]literally, But having heard this ...
[16]ζωῆς was omitted after ἀνάστασιν in the first printing.

(aorist active subjunctive) τὸ θέλημα τοῦ πέμψαντός με[17] καὶ τελειώσω (aorist active subjunctive) αὐτοῦ τὸ ἔργον (= my food is that I may do the will of the one who sent me and fulfil his work).)

page 200 *(top)*

1. ...so that I may pursue (once) (aorist). 2. ...so that I may pursue (more than once) *or* so that I may go on pursuing (present). 3. ...so that you may disturb (more than once) *or* so that you may go on disturbing (present). 4. ...so that you may disturb (once) (aorist). 5. ...so that he/she may ask (once) (aorist). 6. ...so that he/she may ask (several times) *or* ...so that he/she may go on asking (present). 7. ... so that we may write (on this occasion) (aorist). 8. ...so that we may write (more than once) *or* ...so that we may go on writing (present). 9. ...so that you may send out (more than once) *or* so that you may go on sending out (present). (plural) 10. ... so that you may send out once (aorist). (plural) 11. ... so that they may fill (once) (aorist). 12. ... so that they may fill (more than once) *or* so that they may go on filling (present).

(bottom of page)

1.Whenever I see... 2....so that you (singular) may not believe
3.If they cut the trees down...
4.If he/she does not lead the crowd astray...
5. ... so that they may not honour the prophet.
6.If the hired man (once) sees the wolf coming, he will run away.
7.If the hired man sees the wolf coming (generally speaking), he runs away.

page 201

My food is that I may do the will of the one who sent me.
He says to Philip, "Where are we to buy loaves from?"
No one can come to me if the Father who sent me[18] does not draw him.
If I do not wash you (even once), you[19] have no share with me.
The Pharisees heard the crowd muttering this about him, and the high priests and the Pharisees sent out attendants to arrest him.

page 202

Whatever he says to you, do it! (plural)
Go away, call your husband.

---

[17]see *An Introduction to New Testament Greek*, p. 201
[18]literally, the having-sent-me father ...
[19]singular

Father, glorify your name.
Lord, show the father to us.
Remain in me and I (will remain) in (among) you.[20]
If this is what you are doing, reveal yourself to the world.
pages 202-203
They began to ask him to remain beside them.
So they were seeking again to arrest him.
Where I am going, you[21] cannot follow me now.

Optional exercise:
1.τα προβατα ἀποκτεινας ὁ λυκος αὐτα ἀπο της αὐλης ἡρεν.
2.το πλοιον βλεψασα ἡ παιδισκη ἐβοησεν.
3.ἰδου τρια ἐτη ἀφ᾽ οὐ ἐρχομαι ζητων καρπον ἐν τῃ συκῃ ταυτῃ και οὐχ εὑρισκω· ἐκκοψον οὐν αὐτην.
4.τις γαρ ἐξ ὑμων θελων πυργον οἰκοδομησαι οὐχι πρωτον καθισας ψηφιζει την δαπανην;
5.οὐτοι οἱ ἐσχατοι μιαν ὡραν ἐποιησαν, και ἰσους ἡμιν αὐτους ἐποιησας τοις βχστασασι το βαρος της ἡμερας και τον καυσωνα.
6.λεγει τῳ ἀνθρωπῳ· ἐκτεινον την χειρα. και ἐξετεινεν.

---

[20]Understanding μενῶ after κἀγὼ (= καὶ ἐγὼ), and the equivalent of "if so" before ἐγὼ. Barrett, p.474, would prefer to understand μένω (subjunctive) after κἀγὼ: "remain in me, and let me remain in you".
[21]singular

Section 26

page 207
1.I ate. 2.You took. (singular) 3.Did he/she/it throw? 4.We drank. 5.You found. (plural) 6.The prophets died. 7.Did you (singular) bring the sheep? 8.What did the shepherd say? 9.We had no bread (*literally*, we had not bread (at that precise time)). 10.The priest came. 11.We saw a hundred ships. 12.He (*or* she) is finding the drachma.[1] 13.He (She) found the drachma. 14.He (she) was finding the drachma.[2] 15.The children drank the water. 16.The children were drinking the water.

page208
1.having thrown (nominative singular masculine) 2.throwing (nominative singular masculine) 3.having found (nominative singular feminine) 4.finding (nominative singular feminine) 5.having fallen (nominative or accusative singular neuter). 6.falling (nominative or accusative singular neuter) 7.having eaten (nominative singular masculine) 8.eating (nominative singular masculine) 9.having seen (nominative singular masculine) 10.seeing (nominative singular masculine).
11.The prophet saying this, all the disciples were listening. (=While the prophet was saying this, all the disciples were listening.)
12.The prophet having said this, all the disciples fled. (= When (*or* after) the prophet had said this, all the disciples fled.)

page 209 - *infinitives*
1.present 2.aorist 3.aorist 4.present 5.present 6.aorist 7.present 8.aorist 9.aorist[3] 10.present 11.present 12.aorist.

Imperatives
1.aorist 2.present 3.present 4.aorist 5.present 6.aorist 7.aorist 8.present 9.aorist[4] 10.present.

---

[1]εὑρίσκει is present.
[2]ηὕρισκε and ἔπινε (sentence 16) are both imperfect.
[3]Weak aorist.
[4]Weak aorist (2nd person singular) *An Introduction to New Testament Greek* (p.201).

Section 26

page 210 - *subjunctives*
1.aorist 2.present 3.present 4.aorist 5.aorist 6.present 7.aorist[5]
8.present 9.present. 10.aorist.

1. ... so that they may not die. 2.If he/she comes ... 3.If we don't come ...
4.Whenever they see ... 5.Take! (*or* receive!) (singular) 6.Drink! (plural)
7.Lead the lamb into the sheepfold. 8.To have. 9.To eat. 10.Take that!
(plural) 11.Look![6] 12.To lead. 13.To throw. (once) 14.To throw.
(generally). 15.To die.[7]

pages 210-211
For the sake of this[8] I came baptizing with water.
And having made a whip out of ropes he threw (them) all out of the temple.
Therefore they said to him, "What are we to do so that we may do the
work[9] of God?"
They said to him, "What miracle are you doing, then, so that we may see
and come to believe in you? What work are you doing? Our fathers ate
manna in the desert."
Jesus heard that they threw[10] him outside, and having found him said to
him, "Do you trust (*or* believe in) the son of God?"
Therefore when Jesus (had) said "I am he", they drew back[11] and fell on the
ground.

page 212
1.The true prophet. 2.Of the true disciples. 3.What is the truth? (*literally*,
What is the true thing?) 4.This farmer is a kinsman of the king. 5.He will
give the book to the true disciples.

---

[5]Both 7 and 10 are weak aorist subjunctive.

[6]Although a singular imperative, ἴδε is sometimes used when addressing more than one
person, as in John XI, 36 ἴδε πῶς ἐφίλει αὐτόν (Look how he loved him!), which is
obviously addressed to the public of Bethany in general.

[7]A single occurrence, as compared with ἀποθνήσκειν, to die (or "death") in general.

[8]i.e. For this reason ...

[9]See p. 68 above, footnote 1.

[10]Notice that the natural English here is "had thrown". Greek often has the aorist where
we should expect a pluperfect in English (see *An Introduction to New Testament Greek*,
section 30, p.267).

[11]So Zerwick and Grosvenor; literally, "they went away to the rear."

page 213
1.truly 2.wickedly 3.well (*or* beautifully, finely, nobly) 4.similarly (likewise) 5.otherwise (differently).

pages 213-214
Jesus saw Nathanael coming towards him, and says about him, "Look, truly an Israelite in whom there is not deceit."

He said to him, "Because I said to you, 'I saw you underneath the fig tree', do you believe (in me)?"

The one who has received his testimony has set his seal (to the fact) that God is true.

Says one of the slaves of the high priest, being a kinsman of (the man) whose ear Peter (had) cut off, "Didn't I see you in the garden with him?"

page 215
1.They went up. 2.We went down. 3.Having gone across, *or* having changed over. (nominative singular masculine) 4.Go down! (singular) 5.(Of) the woman having gone down. (Probably genitive absolute: = After the woman had gone down.) 6.To go across *or* to change over (once).

pages 215-216
Therefore Pilate went again into the praetorium, and called Jesus, and said to him, "Are you the king of the Jews?"

So then the other disciple, the one who had come first to[12] the tomb, went in too, and saw and came to believe.

And meanwhile[13] his disciples came and began to be surprised because he was speaking with a woman; however, no one said "What do you want?" or "Why are you speaking with her?"

pages 217-218
So a great crowd of the Jews knew that he was there, and they came not because of Jesus only but so that they might also see Lazarus, whom he raised from the dead.[14]

And those (angels) say to her, "Lady, why do you weep?" She says to them, "They took away my Lord, and I do not know where they put him."

---

[12]εἰς sometimes, as here, means "near" rather than "into".

[13]ἐπὶ τούτῳ, "on this", here means "during this time", i.e., "meanwhile" (Bauer).

[14]Literally, "from among corpses". This is a regularly-used formula.

But as (when) his brothers (had) gone up to the festival, then he himself also went up, not openly, but in secret.

And already the festival being half over,[15] Jesus went up into the temple and began to teach.

His disciples went down to[16] the sea.

A woman comes from Samaria to draw water. Jesus says to her, "Give me (something) to drink."

Truly, truly I say to you, the one who believes [in me] has everlasting life. I am the bread of life. Your fathers ate manna in the desert and died. This is the bread (which is) coming down out of heaven, so that a person may eat (some) of it and may not die. I am the living bread, the one who has come down[17] out of heaven; if any one eats (some) of this bread he will live for ever. And the bread, furthermore,[18] which I shall give, is my flesh, [which I shall give] on behalf of the life of the world.

So Jesus having got to know that they were (are)[19] intending to come and seize him so that they may (might) make him king, retreated again towards[20] the mountain, himself alone.

Optional exercise:

1. καὶ οὐκ ἔφαγεν οὐδὲν ἐν ταῖς ἡμέραις ἐκείναις.

2. ὁ δὲ Ἰησοῦς εἶπεν αὐτοῖς· οὐ χρείαν ἔχουσιν ἀπελθεῖν, δότε αὐτοῖς ὑμεῖς φαγεῖν.

3. καταβάντος δὲ αὐτοῦ ἀπο τοῦ ὄρους ἠκολούθησαν αὐτῷ ὄχλοι πολλοι.

4. καὶ ιδου λεπρος προσελθων προσεκυνει αὐτῷ λεγων· κυριε, ἐὰν θελῃς δυνασαι με καθαρισαι.

---

[15]i.e. When the festival was already half over ...

[16]ἐπί + accusative "on", "over", often means "to the neighbourhood of" (v. Bauer, p.288 (ἐπί III γ).

[17]"the having-come-down-one"

[18]δὲ here introduces a fresh thought (Barrett, *The Gospel acording to St. John*, p.297.)

[19]For the tense of μέλλουσιν, see p.77 above.

[20]See εἰς, in the appendix to section 8 of *An Introduction to New Testament Greek* .

page 220
1.I answered 2.You noticed. (singular) 3.He/she/it began. 4.Did we have a wash? 5.You gave orders. (plural) 6.They healed. 7.Did you begin? (singular) 8.Didn't you have a wash? (plural) 9.We chose. 10.He/she/it noticed. 11.I am sending.[1] 12.You answered.[2] (singular)

13.The prophet chose the (*or* his) disciples.
14.The disciples healed the maidservant.
15.The priests denied this.
16.We noticed the farmers working.
17.We were watching[3] the farmers working.
18.Did you give orders to the shepherd to bring the lamb?
19.When the lad asked this, the doorkeeper didn't reply.

page 222
1.He/she/it was destroyed. 2.You became (*or* you happened). (singular) 3.He/she/it arrived. 4.We were arriving. 5.You were destroyed. (plural) 6.Did they become? (*or* Did they happen?)

7.The carpenter became blind.
8.The cities were destroyed.
9.Where did you arrive from? (singular)

(a)The prophet became lame (all of a sudden - aorist) *and* The prophet was getting lame (imperfect).

(b)The maidservants were arriving (imperfect) *and* The maidservants arrived (aorist).

(c)You became (aorist, second person singular) *and* You were becoming (imperfect, second person singular).

(d)They were being destroyed (imperfect passive) *and* They were destroyed (then and there)(aorist middle).

(e)The wind was becoming great (imperfect) *and* The wind became great (aorist).

---

[1] 1st person singular, present active
[2] 2nd person singular, aorist middle (NB, augment)
[3] Imperfect.

Section 27

And on the third day a wedding happened in Cana in[4] Galilee.
You did not choose me, but I chose you.
This happened in Bethany beyond Jordan, where John was, baptising.
page 223
1.having given orders (nominative masculine singular) 2.having denied *or* refused (nominative masculine singular) 3.having chosen (nominative masculine singular) 4.having arrived (nominative masculine singular).
5.The maidservant, having had a wash, went down towards the temple.
6.Having noticed the wolves, the shepherds were becoming troubled.
7.The wind having become great (i.e. because the wind had become great) the disciples began to be afraid.
8.The Jews see that the disciples have healed the lame man.[5]
page 224
1.To begin. 2.To arrive. 3.To be destroyed. 4.To give orders. 5.To deny (*or* refuse). 6.To heal. 7.To choose.
8.No one could observe the lamb.
9.The Pharisees were not willing to heal the lame man on the Sabbath.
10.The prophet gave orders to the lame man to have a wash in the pool.
11.The disciple does not want to deny this.
12.They cannot arrive on the first day.
page 225
1.Begin! (singular) 2.Observe! (plural) 3.Let him/her/it give orders.
4.Let them heal. 5.Arrive! (plural) 6.Let him/her/it be destroyed.
7.Refuse! (*or* deny!) (plural) 8.Let them have a wash. 9.Choose! (singular) 10.Arrive! (singular)
11.Arrive early! 12.Have a wash, o priests! 13.Don't become wicked (men).
14.Don't become a slave of your desires.
15.May the works of sin be destroyed!
16.Let the disciples not begin to fight among themselves.
17.Whenever the prophet calls, arrive early at the temple.
18.Behold the deeds of your fathers!
19.Choose twelve men; lead them across the Jordan.
20.(Always) help the lame, (now) heal the sick.

---

[4]See p. 91 above, footnote 5.
[5]literally, "The Jews see the having-healed-the-lame-man disciples."

And he said to him, "Go away, have a wash in the pool of Siloam" ... so he went away and washed himself, and came seeing.

pages 226-7

1. ... so that I may arrive. 2. ... so that he/she/it may begin. 3. ... so that you may not notice. 4. ... so that they may have a wash. 5.If he/she/it chooses you ... 6.If they don't heal the lame man ... 7.Whenever we observe this ... 8.Whenever he/she/it doesn't give you orders to do this ...

9.Whenever we deny this, no one believes us.

10.I shall go to the pool so that I may have a wash.

11.The old man will flee from the country so that he may not observe these things.

12.If the shepherd arrives, give him orders to bring the sheep into the sheepfold.

pages 227-228

For in this way did God come to value[6] the world that he (actually) gave his only-begotten son, so that each believer in him might not be destroyed, but might have everlasting life.

He was in the world, and the world happened by means of him, and the world did not know him.

And the word became flesh and took up residence[7] among us, and we noticed its[8] glory, glory as of the only-begotten from beside the father, full of grace and truth.

And this is the testimony of John, when the Jews sent priests and Levites from Jerusalem so that they might ask him, "Who are you?" and he told (them) plainly "I am not the Christ" and did not deny (it).

Look, I am saying to you, lift up your eyes and notice that the fields are white for harvest.

Didn't I choose you twelve? And out of you, one is a devil.

If any one keeps my word, for all time he will not experience death.

---

[6]or "delight in".

[7]literally, "pitched its tent". Notice the aorist tense.

[8]or "his". The Greek word αὐτοῦ refers back to ὁ λόγος ("the word") which is, of course, masculine in Greek but not in English. "His" and "its" are therefore, in this context, represented by the same word (αὐτοῦ) in Greek.

Section 27

1.more wicked 2.more similar 3.healthier 4.blinder 5.truer.
6.The king is more wicked than the high priest.
Truly, truly I am saying to you, when you were younger, you used to dress
yourself and you used to walk about where you wanted.
Whoever would receive this child in connection with my name, receives
me; and whoever receives me, receives the one who has sent me; for the
younger[9] among all of you, this is the one who is great.

Optional exercise:
1.ὁ δε ἠρνησατο λεγων· οὐκ οἰδα αὐτον, γυναι.
2.και καταβαινοντων αὐτων ἐκ του ὀρους ἐνετειλατο αὐτοις ὁ
Ἰησους.
3.και ἠλθον εἰς Καφαρναουμ. και ἐν τη οἰκια γενομενος ἐπηρωτα
αὐτους· τι ἐν τη ὁδῳ διελογιζεσθε;
4.τουτων δε πορευομενων ἠρξατο ὁ Ἰησους λεγειν τοις ὀχλοις περι
Ἰωαννου· τι ἐξηλθατε εἰς την ἐρημον θεασασθαι; καλαμον ὑπο
ἀνεμου σαλευομενον;
5.και ἐπιλαβομενος ἰασατο αὐτον και ἀπελυσεν.
6.οἱ υἱοι του αἰωνος τουτου φρονιμωτεροι ὑπερ τους υἱους του φωτος
εἰς την γενεαν την ἑαυτων εἰσιν.

---

[9]μικρότερος corresponds to μείζων in verse 46 (εἰσῆλθεν δὲ διαλογισμὸς ἐν αὐτοῖς,
τὸ τίς ἂν εἴη μείζων αὐτῶν (*literally,* a controversy ensued among them, namely,
who of them might be greater)). Both RSV and the New International Version translate
μείζων as "greatest" and μικρότερος as "least",and Bauer cites Luke IX, 46-48 as a
passage where comparatives are used with the meaning of superlatives. Moulton (p.305)
suggests that μείζων is used here because μέγιστος would have implied three or four
degrees of rank among the Twelve. In some cases, it is uncertain whether the
comparative is used with the meaning of a superlative: at Acts XVII 22, both RSV and
NIV translate δεισιδαιμονεστέρους as "very religious", making it equivalent to a
superlative; but it is possible that ἄλλων is understood, and then St. Paul's meaning is
"I observe that you Athenians are more religious than other (people)"; if so, the meaning
of δεισιδαιμονεστέρους is comparative. (μικρός can mean "little" referring to age or to
importance; see Bauer, p.521.)

Section 28

page 232 (*top*)
1. I was troubled.[1] 2.You were glorified. (singular) 3.He/she/it was loosed. 4.We were hidden. 5.You were troubled. (plural) 6.They were glorified.
7.Was the prophet saved?
8.Weren't the blind man's parents troubled?
(*bottom*)
1.I was not awakened. 2.Were you left behind? (singular)
3.Lazarus was raised from the dead.
4.We were left behind in the desert.
5.Were you (plural) left behind by the bandits?
6.They were awakened at the first hour.

page 233
1.I was frightened. 2.You were born. (singular) 3.He/she was crucified.
4.We were called. 5.They were filled.
6.The truth was revealed. 7.Were the water pots filled?
8.The good (noble) shepherd was not frightened.

page 234
1.Did you remember? (plural) 2.You turned round. (singular) 3.He/she proceeded into the garden. 4.We replied to the priest. 5.They all remembered his words. 6.They turned round towards the king.
(*revision*)
1.Were you saved? (plural) 2.He/she/it was troubled. 3.Were the shepherds awakened? 4.The sheep were frightened.
5.The maidservant filled[2] the water pots.
6.The water pots were filled by the maidservant.
7.The truth was revealed by your fathers.
8.The priest turned back towards the temple.

---

[1]It is important to see the difference in all of the following examples between what the aorist passive means and what the imperfect passive would have meant, e.g. between the aorist passive ἐταράχθην ("I was troubled on a particular occasion", or "I became troubled (just then)" and the imperfect passive ἐταρασσόμην ("I was troubled (during that time)" or "I was being troubled").
[2]Aorist active.

9. What did you reply to the king?
10. The sea was troubled by the wind.
11. The doorkeeper wasn't frightened.
12. The shepherd wasn't frightened, was he?
13. We were called thieves by the scribes and Pharisees.

pages 235-6

And both Jesus and (his) disciples were invited to the wedding.

Having said this, Jesus was troubled in the spirit[3] and testified and said, "Truly, truly I am saying to you that one of you will betray me."

And each (man) made his way to his house, but Jesus made his way to the mount of Olives.

But there was in the place where he was crucified a garden, and in the garden a new tomb.

(The word) came to its own things, and its own people did not receive it. But as many as[4] did receive it[5], it gave them authority to become children of God, to those believing in his name, and (it was) not from blood(s)[6] nor from will[7] of flesh nor from will of man but from God (that) they were born.

So the Jews answered and said to him, "What sign do you show to us because[8] you are doing this? Jesus answered and said to them, "Pull down[9] this temple and inside three days I shall raise it up. So the Jews said, "This

---

[3]This is taken to mean "his spirit". See Barrett, *The Gospel according to St. John*, p.445.

[4]literally, "how many received it..."

[5]See footnote on page 100.

[6]See Bauer, p.22, and Barrett, *The Gospel acording to St. John*, p.164. Blood was sometimes thought to be involved in procreation, and the plural is probably used because the blood of both the father and the mother is meant.

[7]Bauer gives as the meaning of τὸ θέλημα "what is willed", what one wishes to happen. It is often used for the will of God. In I Corinthians VII, 37, St. Paul uses the same word for sexual desire: ὃς ... ἐξουσίαν ἔχει περὶ τοῦ ἰδίου θελήματος = who ... has control of his own (sexual) desire; this, some think, is the contrasting meaning of ἐκ θελήματος ἀνδρὸς here.

[8]"to account for (your doing this)" (Zerwick & Grosvenor).

[9]literally, "undo ... "

temple in forty six years was built,[10] and will you raise it inside three days?" But *he* was speaking about the temple of his body. So when he was raised from the dead, his disciples remembered that he used to say this, and believed in the scripture and in the word that Jesus said.

So the Jews did not believe about him that he was blind and received[11] his sight, until they called the parents of the very man who had received his sight and asked them, saying, "Is this your son, (about) whom you say that he was born blind? So how (is it that) he now sees?" So his parents answered and said, "We know that this is our son and that he was born blind; but how he now sees, we do not know; neither who opened his eyes do we know; ask him, he is grown up, he himself about himself will speak."

page 238

1.having been troubled (nominative masculine singular) 2.having been loosened *or* undone (nominative masculine singular) 3.having been left behind (nominative masculine singular) 4.having been awakened (nominative feminine singular) 5.having proceeded (nominative feminine singular) 6.having turned round (nominative or accusative neuter singular).

7.Having been awakened by the maidservant, the doorkeeper opened the temple.

8.Having been born in Judaea, they worship in Jerusalem.

---

[10]Barrett, *The Gospel according to St. John* p.200, translates: "This sanctuary was built in forty six years". He explains the dative partly as "locative" (at a period of 46 years, regarding the whole period as a single unit) and partly as instrumental (by the lapse of forty six years). There is a historical difficulty, noted by Barrett, that Josephus, *The Antiquities of the Jews*, says (xv, 380) that building began in 20/19 B.C., and was not finished until A.D.63. Barrett suggests either that "grammar must be strained" so that the meaning can be "building has been going on for 46 years (and is still in progress)" or that building had been temporarily stopped, or that St. John mistakenly supposed the temple to be complete at this time.

[11]ἀναβλέπω (see *An Introduction to New Testament Greek*, p.194) means both "I look up" and "I see again", but Bauer notices (pp.50-1) that it is used not only of people who have lost their sight and regain it (like St. Paul at Acts IX, 12) but also of people who have never been able to see; so that it means not only "I regain my sight" but also "I receive my sight", "I become able to see". Bauer cites a non-biblical instance from Pausanias, *Description of Greece*, IV, xii, 10: συνέβη δὲ καὶ Ὀφιονέα τὸν μάντιν τοῦτον, τὸν ἐκ γενετῆς τυφλόν, ἀναβλέψαι παραλόγως δὴ μάλιστα ἀνθρώπων (= and it happened also that Ophioneus, this seer, who was blind from birth, received his sight in the most remarkable way).

9.We do not understand the writings revealed by this prophet.
10.They put the water pot filled with wine in the courtyard.

But having turned round and having noticed them following, Jesus says to them, "What are you looking for?"
Jesus says to her, "Mary." Having turned round, *she* says to him in Hebrew, "Rabboni" (which means[12]"master").

Infinitives.
1.To be glorified. 2.To be hidden. 3.To be awakened. 4.To be left behind. 5.To be frightened (*or* to fear). 6.To be crucified. 7.To be called. 8.To answer. 9.To remember.
page 239
Nicodemus says to him, "How can a man be born, being old?"
And just as Moses raised the snake up in the desert, so must the son of man be raised up, so that every believer in him may have everlasting life.

Imperatives
1.Be hidden! (plural) 2.Answer! (plural) 3.Let them be left behind. 4.Remember! (singular) 5.Let your joy be made clear.

Leave your gift there ... and go away first, be reconciled with your brother.
page 241
1. ... so that the water pot may be filled. 2.Whenever the disciples make their way ... 3. ... so that we may not be left behind. 4.If you are troubled ... (plural) 5.If they are not hidden ... 6.Whenever they don't remember ... 7.How are we to be saved?
pages 241-2
The sick man replied to him, "Lord, I don't have a man so that, at such time as the water is disturbed, he may put me into the pool."
His disciples asked him saying, "Rabbi, who sinned, this man or his parents, so that he should be born blind?" Jesus answered, "Neither did this man sin

---

[12]literally, "is called".

107

nor his parents, but (it was) so that the works of God should be made clear in him."

For God did not send his son into the world so that he might judge the world, but so that the world might be saved through him.

Every evil-doer[13] hates the light and does not come towards the light, so that his deeds may not be shown up.

But Jesus, having heard, said, "This illness is not towards death, but on behalf of the glory of God, so that the son of God may be glorified through it."

Then, therefore, he handed him over to them so that he might be crucified.

Jesus answered and said to him, "Truly, truly I am saying to you, if a person[14] is not born from above (*or* all over again) he cannot see the kingdom of heaven. Nicodemus says to him, "How can a man be born when he is old? He can't enter into his mother's belly a second time and be born, can he?" Jesus answered, "Truly, truly I am saying to you, if a person is not born out of water and spirit, he cannot come into the kingdom of God ... Don't be surprised because I said to you, 'You must be born from above (*or* all over again).'"

pages 243-4
I am the true vine, and my father is the farmer. Every branch in me not bearing fruit, he takes this one away, and every branch bearing fruit he prunes it so that it may bear more fruit.

Because I said to you that I saw you underneath the fig tree, do you believe? You will see greater things than these.

The head steward calls the bridegroom and says to him, "Every man first puts the fine wine out, and when they are drunk, the lesser."

Truly, truly, I am telling you, a slave is not greater than his master, nor an apostle[15] greater than the one who sent him.

But I have a greater testimony than John.

---

[13]literally, "every the evil-doing man".

[14]N.B., τις can be both masculine and feminine.

[15]ἀπόστολος and ἀποστέλλω come from the same root; in Greek, this verse sounds like,"the sent-out man is not greater than the having-sent-(him)-out."

Section 28

The queen of the south will be awakened in the judgement with the men of this generation and will condemn[16] them, because she came from the boundaries of the earth to hear the wisdom of Solomon, and see! something greater[17] than Solomon (is) here.

page 245

According to the grace of God having been given to me as a wise master builder I laid the foundation.

Optional exercise:

1.παντες γαρ αὐτον εἰδον και ἐταραχθησαν.

2.Πατερ ἡμων ὁ ἐν τοις οὐρανοις
ἁγιασθητω το ὀνομα σου.

3.τοτε ἀπεκριθησαν αὐτῳ τινες των γραμματεων και Φαρισαιων λεγοντες· διδασκαλε, θελομεν ἀπο σου σημειον ἰδειν.

4.μη κρινετε, ἱνα μη κριθητε.

5.λεγω δε ὑμιν τοις φιλοις μου, μη φοβηθητε ἀπο των ἀποκτεινοντων το σωμα και μετα ταυτα μη ἐχοντων περισσοτερον τι ποιησαι.

6.τοτε ὁ Ἰησους ἀνηχθη εἰς την ἐρημον ὑπο του πνευματος πειρασθηναι ὑπο του διαβολου.

---

[16] or "cause them to be condemned" (Zerwick & Grosvenor). Bauer, p.412, notes that the conduct of one person, since it sets a standard, can result in the condemnation before God of another person.

[17]πολύς can mean "deep", "profound" as well as simply "much" (Bauer, p.688).

<u>page 248</u>
1.Have I written? 2.You have not come to believe. (singular) 3.Hasn't
he/she written? 4.Have we come to believe? 5.You haven't come to
believe. (plural) 6.They have written.
7.The disciples have come to believe in the new (*or* young) prophet.
8.The slave has written the book.
<u>page 249(*top*)</u>
1.I have done this well. 2.You have testified. (singular) 3.Has he/she
spoken? 4.They have become weary. 5.Have you kept the law? (plural)
(*bottom*)
1.The Jews have not come to love the Romans.
2.Have you (singular) come to hate the Samaritan woman?
3.Has the prophet died?
4.We have made friends with[1] the priests. 5.You haven't spoken to the high
priest, have you? 6.The officer's son has not died.
<u>page 250</u>
1.I have descended from the mountain.
2.Have you (singular) seen the new book?
3.He/she has sent the disciples away into the desert.
4.We haven't seen your drachma.
5.Have you sent the children to school?
6.They haven't gone down to the sea yet.
<u>pages 251-252</u>
(a)1.I have understood this.   2.Have you given this to us?
3.He has become blind just now.   4.We have come to the mountain.

5.Have you heard his voice?
6.Why are you standing here? We are waiting for our parents.
7.Why is the doorkeeper's wife rejoicing? Has she found the drachma?
8.In the middle of the city a great fig tree stands; however, no fruit is
found on it, but only leaves.

---

[1]*literally*, We have befriended the priests.

(b) Everything happened through him, and without him happened not even one thing which has happened.

Rabbi,[2] we know that you have come from God (as) a teacher.

And they went to John and said to him, "Rabbi, (the man) who was with you across the Jordan, to whom you have testified, look! he is baptising and all men are going to him."

The father loves (delights in) the son, and has given everything in[3] his hand.

After this, Jesus finds him in the temple and said to him, "Look, you have become healthy, sin no longer, so that something worse may not happen to you."

I have spoken this to you in dark sayings; the time is coming when I shall no longer speak to you in dark sayings, but I shall make a proclamation to you in frankness about the father.

Jesus said this and having lifted up his eyes to[4] heaven he said; "Father, the moment has come; glorify your son, so that the son may glorify you, just as you have given him authority of (= over) all flesh, so that in respect of all[5] those whom you have given to him he may give to them everlasting life. ... I made your name known to the men whom you gave to me out of the world. They were yours and you gave them to me and they have observed (kept) your word."

page 253

1.To have come to believe. 2.To have come to hate. 3.To have become weary. 4.To have become *or* To have happened. 5.To have sent out. 6.To have died. 7.To have understood. 8.To have heard.

page 254

1.having come to believe (nominative masculine singular) 2.having done *or* made (nominative feminine singular) 3.having gone down (nominative

---

[2]Bauer (p. 733) translates ῥαββί as "my lord", a form of address used as an honorary title for outstanding teachers of the law, deriving it from the Hebrew *rab* (= "chief"), and says that διδάσκαλε at John I, 38, is a paraphrase. Perhaps "master" conveys more of the full dignity of **Rabbi**. *The New Brown-Driver-Briggs-Gesenius Hebrew and English Lexicon*, p.912, translates *Rabbi* as "my master, teacher".

[3]We should prefer to say "into", and Bauer notes (p.260) that in Koiné Greek ἐν + dative is sometimes found with verbs implying motion, as "give" does here, instead of εἰς + accusative.

[4]εἰς can indicate a goal to which one aspires (Bauer, p.229).

[5]Taking πᾶν as accusative of respect.

or accusative neuter singular) 4.the things that have happened (the having happened things) (nominative *or* accusative neuter plural) 5.(women) having testified (nominative feminine plural).

6.We proclaim salvation to those who have kept the law (to the having-kept-the-law men).

7.The man who has written this book (the having-written-this-book man) worships in Jerusalem.

8.To those who have come on the first day of the festival (to the having-come-on-the-first-day-of-the-festival men), we shall give one drachma.

9.We cannot find those who have died in the desert (the having-died-in-the-desert men).

10.The maidservant having said this, the bandits fled.

11.The lad having given his testimony, all came to believe.

12.You see that the high priest is tired. (You see the high priest having become weary).

page 255

So Jesus was saying to those Jews who had come to believe in him: "If you remain in my word, truly you are my disciples."

So Jesus, having become weary from his journey, was sitting down.

So the crowd that was standing (there) and that had heard began to say that thunder had occurred (began to say thunder to have occurred).

You have sent away to John, and he has testified to the truth.

That one was a man-slayer from (the) beginning, and does not stand in the truth, because there is not truth in him.

So the Jews said to him, "Now we know (we have come to understand) that you have a devil."

He said to them, "Do you know what I have done to you?"

And no one has gone up into heaven except the one who came down[6] out of heaven, the son of man."

---

[6]the (one) having come down (aorist participle)

112

The one[7] who hears my word and who believes in the one who sent me has everlasting life and is not coming[8] into judgement but has changed over from death to life.
page 257
Truly, truly I am saying to you, in so far as you did (it) to one of these the least of my brothers, you did it to me.

And again he began to teach beside the sea. And there is brought together towards him a very numerous crowd.

So if (there is any one) who breaks one of the least (important) commandments and so teaches men, he will be called least in the kingdom of heaven.

Optional exercise:
1.ταυτα λελαληκα ὑμιν ἱνα μη σκανδαλισθητε.
2.εἰ ὁ κοσμος ὑμας μισει, γινωσκετε ὁτι ἐμε πρωτον ὑμων μεμισηκεν.
3.ἀπο τοτε ἠρξατο ὁ Ἰησους κηρυσσειν και λεγειν· μετανοειτε· ἠγγικεν γαρ ἡ βασιλεια των οὐρανων.
4.ὑπαγε εἰς τον οἰκον σου προς τους σους και ἀπαγγειλον αὐτοις ὁσα ὁ κυριος σοι πεποιηκεν.
5.ὁ ἑωρακως ἐμε ἑωρακεν τον πατερα.
6.ὁ πιστος ἐν ἐλαχιστῳ και ἐν πολλῳ πιστος ἐστιν, και ὁ ἐν ἐλαχιστῳ ἀδικος και ἐν πολλῳ ἀδικος ἐστιν.

---

[7]"The believer is described as ὁ τὸν λόγον μου ἀκούων καὶ πιστεύων τῷ πέμψαντί με." Barrett, *The Gospel according to St John*, p. 261.
[8]Greek sometimes uses a forward-looking present for a future, like the English "I am going on holiday tomorrow".

Section 30

page 260
1.Have I been led? 2.Have you been judged? (singular) 3.He/she/it has been written. 4.We have not been judged. 5.Haven't you been led? (plural) 6.The letters have been sent.
7.The bandits have been judged by the great king.
8.Has the woman's name been written in the book?
9.Have we been led to the temple of the true god?
10.You haven't been led up the garden by the maidservant, have you?

page 261
1.I have been shut in the temple.
2.A child has been born in Judaea.
3.Has all the work (have all the deeds) been finished?
4.We have been sent out to the land of our fathers.
5.You (plural) have been betrayed into the hands of the bandits.
6.The hands of the bandits have been bound.
7.The palsied (men) haven't been cured, have they?

page 262[1]
1.How has this happened?
2.On the first day of the festival the miracles have already been revealed.
3.Why have you become disciples of this prophet?
4.We haven't just[2] become rich, have we?

page 263
1.The sick are lying down in the sanctuary.
2.Are you sitting in the courtyard?
3.We are all sitting at dinner eating baked fish.
4.Has the sick man died?
5.What has happened? All the gardeners are lying down on their beds under the fig tree.

I am not going up to this festival, because my appointed time has not yet been fulfilled.

---

[1] γεγένημαι is much rarer than γέγονα. Bauer (p.158) reports that it is only unquestioned at John II, 9 ὡς δὲ ἐγεύσατο ὁ ἀρχιτρίκλινος τὸ ὕδωρ οἶνον γεγενημένον (= but as the head steward tasted the water having become wine...)
[2] just now

Section 30

So the Pharisees replied to them, "You haven't been led astray as well, have you?"

And furthermore (δὲ) in your law it has been written that the testimony of two men is true.

So they said to him, "We have not been born out of[3] prostitution."

He said this, and after this he says to them, "Our friend Lazarus has died."

Both all my things are yours and yours mine, and I have been glorified in them.

The ruler of this world has been judged.

Now my soul has become troubled.

page 266

There occurred a man (having been) sent out from (beside) God, (and) his name (was) John.

The thing that has been[4] born out of flesh is flesh; and the thing that has been born out of the spirit is spirit.

It is (a thing that has been) written in the prophets, "And they shall all be God's instructed (ones)."[5]

His disciples remembered that it is something written,[6] "The zeal of your house will devour me."

Ask and you will receive, so that your joy may be filled (may be having-been-filled).

And he went into the tomb, and notices (that) the linen cloths (are) lying (there), and the handkerchief which was over his head, not lying with the other cloths but wrapped up separately into one place.

---

[3]i.e., as a result of

[4]having been born

[5]Barrett notes (*The Gospel according to St John* p.296) that this curious expression is probably a quotation from Isaiah LIV, 12-13 (Septuagint): καὶ θήσω τὰς ἐπάλξεις σου ἴασπιν καὶ τὰς πύλας σου λίθους κρυστάλλου καὶ τὸν περίβολόν σου λίθους ἐκλεκτοὺς καὶ πάντας τοὺς υἱούς σου διδακτοὺς θεοῦ καὶ ἐν πολλῇ εἰρήνῃ τὰ τέκνα σου (= and I shall make (*literally,* put) your parapets of jasper and your gates of diamonds and your encircling wall of choice stones and all your sons God's instructed ones and in great peace your children). Moulton (p.236), translating like this, classifies θεοῦ as a subjective genitive and points out that διδακτοὺς θεοῦ is equivalent to "taught by God", though this does not preserve the flavour of the quotation from Septuagint.

[6]i.e. in the scriptures. Barrett *The Gospel according to St John*, p.198, notes that it is a quotation from Psalm 69 (68, Septuagint), verse 10 (which actually has κατέφαγεν).

Section 30

So Jesus took the loaves and having given thanks he distributed them to those who were his guests at dinner (those reclining).
So the Jews were beginning to say to the man who had been cured, "It is Sabbath, and it is not authorised for you to take up your bed."
<u>page 267</u>
A container was standing (had been put) (there) full of sour wine.
But there is in Jerusalem near the Sheep Gate a pool which is called in Hebrew Bethzatha, having five porches. In these lay down a multitude of the sick, blind, lame (and) palsied.
<u>page 269</u>
But many (out) of the Jews had come to Martha and Mary so that they might console them about their brother.
But Jesus raised his eyes upwards and said, "Father, I thank you because you listened to me. But I knew that you always listen to me. But I said (that) because of the crowd (that is) standing around, so that they may come to believe that you sent me out. And having said this he shouted with a loud voice, "Lazarus, over here! outside!" The dead man[7] came out bound with respect to his feet and hands with grave clothes, and his face had been bound round with a handkerchief.

Optional exercise:
1.και ειπεν·   τουτο ποιησω, καθελω μου τας ἀποθηκας και μειζονας οἰκοδομησω και συναξω ἐκει παντα τον σιτον και τα ἀγαθα μου και ἐρω τη ψυχη μου· ψυχη, ἐχεις πολλα ἀγαθα κειμενα εἰς ἐτη πολλα.
2.ἰδου, οὑτος κειται εἰς πτωσιν και ἀναστασιν πολλων ἐν τω Ἰσραηλ.
3.μακαριοι οἱ δεδιωγμενοι ἑνεκεν δικαιοσυνης, ὁτι αὐτων ἐστιν ἡ βασιλεια των οὐρανων.
4.ἡ δε πενθερα Σιμωνος κατεκειτο πυρεσσουσα, και εὐθυς λεγουσιν αὐτω περι αὐτης.
5.και ὀντος αὐτου ἐν Βηθανια ἐν τη οἰκια Σιμωνος του λεπρου, κατακειμενου αὐτου ἠλθέ γυνη.
6.και ἀπηλθον και εὑρον πωλον δεδεμενον προς θυραν ἐξω ἐπι του ἀμφοδου και λυουσιν αὐτον.   και τινες των ἐκει ἐστηκοτων ἐλεγον αὐτοις· τι ποιειτε λυοντες τον πωλον;

---

[7]the having died (man)

Susanna

1. And there was a man living in Babylon, and his name (was) Ioakim. 2. And he took a wife whose name (was) Susanna, daughter of Khelkios, (and she was) exceedingly beautiful and fearing the Lord. 3. And her parents (were) righteous and taught their daughter according to the law of Moses. 4. And Ioakim was exceedingly rich and had[1] a garden neighbouring his house; and the Jews used to approach him because he was more esteemed than any one.[2] 5. And there were proclaimed two elders out of the people (as) judges during that year, concerning whom the Lord[3] spoke (saying) that lawlessness broke out from Babylon, from the elders (who were) judges, who seemed to govern the people. 6. These men used to work persistently in Ioakim's house, and all those (who were) being judged used to come to them. 7. And it happened that at a time when the people used to depart for the middle of the day,[4] Susanna used to make her way in and walk about in her husband's garden. 8. And the two elders used to observe her coming into the garden day by day[5] and walking about, and they began to desire her.[6] 9. And they distorted their own mind(s) and turned their eyes aside so as not to look into the heaven nor to remember righteous judgements. 10. And they were both smitten concerning her and did not tell each other of their mental agony, 11 because they were ashamed to announce their desire because they wanted to make love with her. 12. And they watched emulously day by day (for an opportunity) to see her. 13. And the one said to the other, "Now then, let us go home, because it is time for lunch;[7] and having gone out, they separated from each other; 14 and having turned back they came to the same (place) and asking each other the reason they admitted their desire; and then in common they arranged a

---

[1]there was to him a garden ...
[2]*literally,* than all (for this genitive, see *An Introduction to New Testament Greek* (to which all following references are made unless shown otherwise), section 27, p.228).
[3]Septuagint sometimes uses δεσπότης for God instead of κύριος (see Bauer).
[4]accusative of time "how long".
[5]καθ᾿ ἡμέραν
[6]*literally,* became in desire of her.
[7]*literally,* the time of lunch.

time together when they would[8] be able to find her alone. 15. And it happened in the (time when they were) watching[9] out for a suitable day she came out once just as the day before and the day before that with two maids and desired to bathe in the garden, because it was hot weather; 16 and there was nobody there except the two elders (who were) hidden and watching her closely. 17. And she said to the maids, "Now then, bring olive oil and soap for me and close the doors of the garden, so that I may bathe." 18. And they did just as she said and closed the doors of the garden and went out by the side doors to bring the things that they had been instructed[10] and they did not see the elders because they were hidden. 19. And it happened that the maids went out and the two old men stood up and attacked her 20 and said "Look, the doors of the garden have been closed and no one is observing us and we are in desire of you; therefore assent to us and become (= make love)[11] with us; 21 but if not, we shall testify against you that there was with you a young man and because of this you sent the maids away from you." 22. And Susanna uttered a groan and said, "I am in a tight corner in every way;[12] for if I do these things, it is death to me, and if I do not do them, I shall not escape (from) your hands; 23 I must choose not having done (them) to fall into your hands (rather) than to sin before the Lord." 24. And Susanna raised a cry in a loud voice, and the two old men also raised a cry in opposition to her. 25. And having run, the one opened the doors of the garden. 26. But as those from the house heard the screaming in the garden, they burst in through the side doors to see the thing (that had) happened to her. 27. But when the old men said their speeches the slaves were exceedingly ashamed, because never had such a word been spoken about Susanna.

28. And it happened the next day, when the people had[13] come together to her husband Ioakim, the two old men came full of the lawless intention

---

[8]*literally*, will.

[9]in the them watching

[10]*literally*, that had been instructed to them.

[11]taking γένου as short for συγγένου (footnote 18 in the text)

[12]*literally*, things are tight for me from all directions.

[13]for the Greek use of an aorist after "when" see section 30, p.267.

against Susanna of killing[14] her 29 and they said in front of the people "Send for Susanna the daughter of Khelkios, who is the wife of Ioakim"; and they sent (for her). 30. And she herself came and her parents and her children and all her relations; 31 and Susanna was very dainty and fair in appearance[15]. 32 But the criminals ordered her to be unveiled, for she had worn her veil down, so that they might be filled with her beauty. 33.But all those beside her and all those who had seen her were weeping. 34. But having stood up in the middle of the people the two old men put their hands on her head; 35 but she, weeping, looked up towards heaven, because her heart was trusting in the Lord. 36. And the old men said, "While we were walking about[16] in the garden alone, this woman came in with two maids and shut the doors of the garden and dismissed the maids; 37 and there came towards her a young man, who had been hidden, and he lay down with her. 38. But we being in the corner of the garden and having seen the offence[17] ran upon them; 39 and having seen them making love, him[18] on the one hand we were unable to get the better of through him being stronger than us, and because he had leapt out, having opened the doors, 40 but having caught hold of this woman we began to ask her who the young man was, 41 and she was unwilling to tell us. These things we testify." And the meeting believed them as elders of the people and judges and condemned her to die. 42. But Susanna called out with a loud voice and said, "Eternal God who has knowledge of the hidden things, the one who knows all things before their creation, 43 you understand that they testified false things of me; and look, I die not having done any of the things in respect of which they acted wickedly against me."

44. And the Lord listened to her voice. 45. And while she was being led away to be killed[19] God raised up the holy spirit of a young lad, whose name was Daniel, 46 and he shouted in a loud voice "I am clean of the blood

[14]*literally*, "the intention of to kill her"

[15]τὸ εἶδος, τοῦ εἴδους = "appearance" (not in footnote to text in 1st printing).

[16]*literally*, "us walking about ..." (genitive absolute).

[17]*literally*, the lawlessness (footnote 9 in the text)

[18]This awkward expression has been left in order to show more clearly the shape of the Greek sentence; it requires reshaping, of course, to become acceptable English.

[19]"and she being led away to be killed" (genitive absolute)

of this woman." 47. And all the people turned round towards him and said "What is this word which you have spoken?" 48. But he, standing in the middle of them said, "(Are you) so foolish, sons of Israel? Not having weighed the evidence or recognised what is clear, did you condemn a daughter of Israel? 49. Turn back to the judgement seat. For these men testified false things against her." 50. And all the people turned back with haste. And the elders said to him, "Sit over here in the middle of us and make a report to us; because God has given you the prerogative." 51. And Daniel said to them, "Separate[20] them far from each other, and I shall judge them." 52.But when they had been separated the one from the other,[21] he called the one of them and said to him, "O man who has grown old (from) evil days, now your sins have come (home to you), that you used to do previously 53 giving unjust verdicts[22] and on the one hand condemning the innocent but on the other setting the guilty free, though the Lord says, '(An) innocent and righteous (person) you shall not kill'; 54 now therefore if indeed you saw this woman, say under what tree you saw them keeping company with each other." And he said, "under a mastic tree." 55. But Daniel said, "You have lied correctly against[23] your own head; for already an angel of God having received the sentence from God will cut[24] you in half." 56. And having set him aside, he ordered (them) to bring the other towards him; and he said to him, "Seed of Canaan and not Judah, beauty deceived you utterly and desire distorted your heart; 57 this is the way you acted to the daughters of Israel, and they, fearing, used to keep company with you, but a daughter of Judah did not submit to your lawlessness; 58 now therefore tell me, under what tree did you catch them keeping company with each other?" And he said, "Under a holm oak."[25] 59. And

---

[20] For διαχωρίζω, see footnote 21 in text.

[21] *literally*, the one from the one

[22] *literally*, judging unjust judgements

[23] Footnote 69 in the text (1st printing) should read εἰς, not ἐπί.

[24] Two puns need to be noticed: The first involves σχῖνος = mastic tree, σχίζω = I cut. If the angel had been going to bite the elder, one would get the same effect with "mastic ... masticate..." (No Hebrew version of Susanna or Bel exists, and so it is not known whether the Hebrew contained puns here also.)

[25] The second pun: πρῖνος = holm oak, πρίω = I cut (really, by sawing). Almost impossible to reproduce in English; perhaps "You saw them under a holm oak? The

Daniel said to him, "You also have lied correctly against your own head; for the angel of God waits, holding a great sword to cut you in half, so that he may destroy you utterly." 60. And all the meeting raised a shout with a loud voice and gave praises to God who saves those who place their hopes in him. 61. And they rose up against the two old men, because Daniel showed out of their (own) mouth (them to be) bearing false witness, and they acted to them in the same way as they had been wicked to their neighbour, 62 to do according to the law of Moses, and they killed them; and guiltless blood was saved on that day. 63. And Chelkias and his wife praised God concerning their daughter Susanna with Ioakim her husband and all their relations, because an unseemly action was not found in her. 64. And Daniel became great in the eyes of the people from that day and thereafter.

Bel and the dragon.

1. From the prophecy of Ambakoum[26] son of Jesus[27] out of the tribe of Levi.

2. There was a certain man (who was) a priest, whose name was Daniel son of Abal, a companion of the king of Babylon. 3. And there was an idol, Bel, which the Babylonians used to worship; and there were used up for it every day 12 artabs of the finest wheaten flour and four sheep and six measures of olive oil. 4. And the king used to worship it, and the king used to go forth every day and bow down to it; but Daniel used to say his prayers to the Lord. 5. And the king said to Daniel, "Why don't you bow down to Bel?" And Daniel said to the king, "I don't worship anyone except the Lord God who established the heaven and the earth and has authority over all flesh." 6. But the king said to him, "Isn't this a god? Don't you see how many things are consumed for him every day?" 7. And Daniel said to him, "By no means let any one cheat you; for this is on the one hand made of mud from the inside, and on the other made of bronze from the outside;

---

angel of God is waiting with a great sword to saw you in half, and you'll never be a whole man again."

[26]The name of Habbakuk in Septuagint, where Bel & the dragon is found at the end of Daniel.

[27]Equivalent to "Joshua".

and I swear to you by the Lord God of gods that this (one)[28] has never eaten anything up. 8. And having become angry the king called those in charge of the temple and said to them "Show me the (person) who eats up the things that are prepared for Bel; but indeed if not, you will die, or (else) Daniel who says that[29] they are not eaten by him." But they said "Bel himself is the one who eats them." 9. And Daniel said to the king, "Let it happen thus; if I do not show you that Bel is not the (one) who eats them, I shall die and all my family." And Bel had[30] 70 priests not counting their wives and children. 10. And they led the king into the idol's temple. 11. And the food was put beside (the idol) in front of the king and Daniel, and wine mixed (with water) (*or* poured out) was brought in and put beside Bel. And Daniel said, "You yourself see that these things have been put down, king; therefore put your seal on the bolts[31] of the temple, at such time as it is closed." 13. And the word pleased the king. 14. But Daniel ordered his household, having thrown[32] every one out of the temple, to strew the whole temple with ash, none of those outside it knowing. And then he ordered (them) to seal the temple with the king's ring and the rings of certain esteemed priests; and so it happened. 15-17. And it happened on the next day they came to[33] the place; but the priests of Bel having entered through secret doors had[34] eaten up all the things that had been put beside Bel and had drunk up the wine. And Daniel said, "Inspect your seals (to see) if they are remaining, priests;[35] and as for you, o king, look (out) lest anything unexpected has happened." And they found that[36] the seal was there, and they took the seal off. 18. And having opened the doors they saw that all the things that had been put beside (Bel) had been consumed[37] and the tables

---

[28]i.e. Bel

[29]Accusative & infinitive construction: who says them not to be eaten ... "

[30]*literally*, there were to Bel ...

[31]κλεῖς means both "key" and "bolt".

[32]i.e. put

[33]*literally*, arrived at

[34]For the use of the aorist in Greek where the pluperfect is usual in English, see *An Introduction to New Testament Greek*, p.267.

[35]ἄνδρες is a little ironical, "gentlemen priests"

[36]ὡς = ὅτι

(were) empty; and the king was glad and said to Daniel, "Great is Bel, and there is no deceit with him." 19. And Daniel laughed exceedingly and said to the king, "(Come) over here, see the deceit of the priests." And Daniel said, "King, whose are these tracks?" And the king said "(They are the tracks) of men and women and children." 21. And he approached the house in which the priests were dwelling, and found the food of Bel and the wine; and Daniel showed the king the secret doors, entering through which the priests used to consume the things put down beside Bel. 22. And the king led them out of the Belium and handed them over to Daniel; and he gave Daniel the expenditure (that was) for him, and he overturned Bel.

23. And there was a dragon in the same place, and the Babylonians used to worship it. 24. And the king said to Daniel, "Surely you won't say that this is made of bronze too? Look, it is alive and eats and drinks; bow down to it." 25. And Daniel said, "King, give me the authority, and I shall kill the dragon without sword and club." 26. And the king reached agreement with him and said to him "It has been given to you." 27. And Daniel, having taken 30 minas of pitch and suet and hair, fastened them together[38] and made a cake and put it into the dragon's mouth, and having eaten[39] it, it burst. And he[40] showed it to the king saying "Don't you worship these things, O king?" 28. And those from the country all joined together against Daniel and said, "Has the king become Jewish? He overturned Bel and killed the dragon." 30. And the king, having seen that the multitude of the country had been gathered together against him, called his companions and said, "I give Daniel to destruction." 31-32. And there was a pit in which 7 lions were kept, to which were delivered those who conspired against the king, and two bodies of those condemned to death were supplied to them every day. And the crowds threw Daniel into that pit, so that he might be eaten up and might not even have a burial place. And Daniel was in the pit for six days. 33.And it happened on the sixth day and Ambakoum

---

[37]literally, all the things having been put beside Bel having been consumed ... After verbs equivalent to "see" or "know", a participle is often used instead of a clause beginning ὅτι.

[38]literally, into the same thing

[39]The subject is now the dragon.

[40]The subject is now Daniel again.

was having bread crumbled in a dish in a hash and a bottle of wine mixed (with water) and was just about to go forth to the plain to the harvesters. 34. And an angel of the Lord spoke to Ambakoum saying "The Lord God says this to you: 'Carry away the breakfast which you have for Daniel into the pit of the lions in Babylon.'" 35. And Ambakoum said, "Lord God, I have not seen Babylon and (as for) the pit, I do not know where it is." 36. And the angel of the Lord, having got hold of Ambakoum by the hair of his head set him above the pit in Babylon. 37. And Ambakoum said to Daniel, "Having got up, eat the breakfast, which the Lord God sent you." 38. And Daniel said, "Well then, the Lord remembered me, the one who does not abandon those who love him." 39. And Daniel ate; but the angel of the Lord replaced Ambakoum where he had taken him (from) on the same day. 40. But after that, the king came out grieving for Daniel and having stooped down (and looked) into the pit, he sees him sitting down. 41. And having raised a cry, the king said "Great is the Lord God, and there is no other (god) except him." 42. And the king brought Daniel out of the pit; and he threw those who were guilty of his destruction into the pit in the sight of Daniel, and they were gobbled up.

Appendix 1 - further grammar

The following list of the most salient topics not covered may be useful to groups which are planning to continue the systematic study of koiné grammar.[1]

Accidence
(a) -μι verbs
φημί and ἔφην (old Attic word for "say yes", "affirm") (found in Matthew, Luke, several epistles and Acts).
ἔστην - strong aorist (intransitive) of ἵστημι also compounds e.g. ἀνθίστημι, ἐξίστημι and καθίστημι. (ἔστην is set out in the conspectus of

---

[1] A check list of essential grammar for inclusion in any first year course in New Testament Greek is given in *Towards Efficient Teaching of New Testament Greek* by Dr. P. Whale, on pp.59-63 of *Classics for Adults*, the report of the conference held at Warwick University in May, 1992.

grammar on p. 334 of *An Introduction to New Testament Greek*, but is not discussed in the main body of the book.)

"Regular" -μι verbs e.g. δείκνυμι, ἀμφιέννυμι and σβέννυμι.

The tendency for -μι verbs to become assimilated to -ω verb forms, e.g. 3rd person plural present of συνίημι ("I understand") is συνίουσιν at Matthew XIII, 13.

εἰμι (future of ἔρχομαι in Attic); found as compounds εἴσειμι, ἔξειμι and ἄπειμι e.g. εἰσῄει at Acts XXI, 18, ἐξιόντων at Acts XIII, 42, and ἀπῄεσαν at Acts XVII, 10.

(b) The use of ἐρῶ as the future active and ἐρρέθην as the aorist passive of λέγω (both found under εἶπον in Bauer).

(c) -υς -εια -υ adjectives. (These are very common in Attic, but not in the New Testament and can safely be deferred. γλυκύ is found at Revelations X 9 and 10; ἡδύς is found only as adverb ἡδέως (also comparative and superlative) in the epistles and Mark; πραΰς is found at Matthew V, 5, XI, 29, and XXI, 5, but not in the feminine. ταχύς is found mainly in the neuter singular ταχύ, used adverbially to mean "soon", "quickly".)

(d) ὅδε ἥδε τόδε (the common Attic demonstrative "this (here)") is frequent in Septuagint introducing prophetic utterances (see Bauer, p. 553) but is only found occasionally in the New Testament; Bauer cites Luke X, 39, Epistle of James IV, 13 and variant readings at Acts XV, 23 and 2 Corinthians XII, 19.

Syntax

Many aspects of koiné syntax repay detailed further study; the following may be particularly important, either to extend the discussion in *An Introduction to New Testament Greek* or because they have only been mentioned in footnotes.

(a) Indirect speech, including indirect statements both with infinitives after verbs of saying and thinking, and with participles after verbs of knowing or perceiving.

(b) The infinitive; both used as noun after τό, e.g. διὰ τὸ μὴ ἔχειν βάθος (Mark IV, 5) (part of reading passage on p. 283 of *An Introduction*

to New Testament Greek), and τοῦ + infinitive meaning "for the purpose of" and many other usages, including ὥστε + infinitive, which differs from the Attic construction. The use of the infinitive with other impersonal verbs as well as δεῖ. (χρή is rare, but συμφέρει, μέλει, πρέπει (sometimes in the form πρέπον ἐστίν) and ἔξεστιν are more common.)
(c) Conditional clauses in general.
(d) Indefinite construction, including ὅστις ἄν.

There are few optatives in NT, as it was dropping out of use. Where it is found, often it is the aorist optative. It is more common in Acts and the epistles than the gospels e.g. Acts VIII, 20 (εἴη - present), Acts XVII, 12 (ἔχοι - present), XVII, 18 (θέλοι - present), XVII, 27 (ψηλαφήσειαν and εὕροιεν - both aorist), Acts XXI, 33 (εἴη -present), Acts XXV, 16 (ἔχοι - present, λάβοι - aorist) and 20 (βούλοιτο - present), Acts XXVI, 29 (εὐξαίμην - aorist), Acts XXVII, 12 and 39 (δύναιντο - present), Romans XV, 5 (δῴη - aorist), 1 Corinthians XV, 37 (τύχοι - aorist, after εἰ)[2], 1 Thessalonians III 11 and 12 (κατευθῦναι,[3] πλεονάσαι, περισσεύσαι - all aorist), V,23 (ἁγιάσαι - aorist), Philemon 20 (ὀναίμην - aorist) 1 Peter I, 2 (πληθυνθείη - aorist)[4] . The most common use of optative in NT is to express a wish, e.g. μὴ γένοιτο - may it not happen! ("God forbid!")(aorist)[5] but it is also used in indirect speech in past sequence. ἵνα + optative is exceedingly rare.

Appendix 2 - An outline guide to Greek accents.

The three kinds of Greek accent are:
′ acute   ` grave   ⁀ circumflex
In Attic (Greek spoken in Athens in the 5th and 4th centuries B.C.) an acute accent indicated a vowel pronounced in a high pitched voice; a grave indicated a vowel pronounced with a low pitched voice, or possibly with the

---

[2] also I Peter III, 14 - πάσχοιτε – present - after εἰ.
[3] also at 2 Thessalonians III, 5.
[4] also at 2 Peter I, 2.
[5] See Bauer, p.158; 13 examples are listed from Paul and 1 from Luke.

voice falling; a circumflex indicated a vowel pronounced at first on a high pitch and then on a lower one.

Acute and grave accents can stand on short or long vowels. The circumflex accent can only stand on a long vowel. ε and ο are always short, η and ω[6] are always long. α, ι, and υ are sometimes long and sometimes short. All diphthongs count as long vowels except that αι and οι are short for the purposes of accentuation when they come at the end of verbs[7] (but αι and οι are long for accentuation when at the end of verbs in the optative).

Normally, each Greek word has one accent, which must be on one of the last three syllables:
an <u>acute</u> accent can be on the third from last syllable, when it is called *proparoxytone*
or on the second from last syllable, when it is called *paroxytone*
or on the last syllable, when it is called *oxytone*.

A <u>circumflex</u> can be on the second from last syllable, when it is called *properispomenon*
or on the last syllable, when it is called *perispomenon*.

A <u>grave</u> accent can only be on the last syllable, when it is called *barytone*.

If the last syllable of a word is short,[8] the accent may be on any of the last three syllables, but if it is long, only on either of the last two.

The barytone accent is only used when there would be an acute accent on the last syllable of a word, and another word follows without any punctuation between, e.g., μαθητής = "disciple" has oxytone accent, but the accent on –ης becomes barytone in μαθητὴς πιστός ("a faithful disciple").

---

[6] A notable exception is the genitive singular of nouns like πόλις and πῆχυς ("cubit"), where ω is counted as short for accentuation, e.g. "of the city" is τῆς πόλεως.

[7] e.g. πέμπομαι, λεγόμενοι

[8] For accentuation, only the vowel length is considered. If a word ends with a short syllable and the accent is on the penultimate, which is long, it is properispomenon.

Appendix (Accents)

The accent on <u>nouns pronouns</u> and <u>adjectives</u> remains according to the form given in the lexicon unless forced to change by the rules. The lexicon form is not always predictable by rule e.g. καλός (beautiful) is oxytone, but φίλος (friendly) is paroxytone: αὐτός is oxytone, but οὗτος is not.

In <u>verbs</u>, the accent is normally as far from the last syllable as possible (e.g., μένω, μένομεν, πιστεύομεν). The following are the main exceptions:

εἰμί, ἐστί and εἰσί and also φημί, φησί

strong aorist active participles are oxytone e.g. λαβών

strong aorist active infinitives have perispomenon e.g. λαβεῖν

strong aorist middle 2nd person imperatives have perispomenon, e.g. γενοῦ.[9]

strong aorist infinitive middle is paroxytone, e.g., γενέσθαι

weak aorist infinitive active is accented on the second syllable from the end, e.g. πιστεῦσαι, γράψαι

perfect active participles are oxytone, e.g. πεπιστευκώς

infinitives ending -ναι are accented on the last syllable but one, e.g. πιστευθῆναι, πεπιστευκέναι[10]

perfect passive and middle participles and infinitives are accented on the last syllable but one, e.g. πεπιστευμένος.

aorist passive participles and active participles of –μι verbs are oxytone e.g. σωθείς and διδούς

the imperatives εἰπέ, ἐλθέ and εὑρέ

The accents of contracted verbs and participles are worked out according to the uncontracted forms; so while the accent on ποιέω (present) becomes ποιῶ in the contracted form, ἐποίεον (imperfect) becomes ἐποίουν.

<u>Enclitics</u> are words which transfer their accents forward to the word in front (see *An Introduction to New Testament Greek* , p.142).

<u>Atona</u> are words without accents. These are: ὁ, ἡ, οἱ, αἱ, εἰς, ἐν, ἐκ, ἐξ, εἰ (= "if"), οὐ, οὐκ, οὐχ, ὡς.

---

[9] ἰδού used as an exclamation is an exception.

[10] P.316 of *An Introduction to New Testament Greek* should be amended.